Now at the Thr

*Tuvia Ruebner*
*1924–2019*

# *Now at the Threshold*

## The Late Poems of
## Tuvia Ruebner

TRANSLATED
by Rachel Tzvia Back

HEBREW UNION COLLEGE PRESS

©Hebrew Union College Press

Library of Congress Cataloging-in-Publication Data

Names: Ruebner, Tuvia, 1924-2019, author. | Back, Rachel Tzvia, 1960-
   translator.
Title: Now at the threshold : the late poems of Tuvia Ruebner / translated
   by Rachel Tzvia Back.
Description: [Cincinnati] : Hebrew Union College Press, [2020] | Summary:
   "The final poems of Israeli poet Tuvia Ruebner, translated and
   introduced by Rachel Tzvia Back"-- Provided by publisher.
Identifiers: LCCN 2019052364 (print) | LCCN 2019052365 (ebook) | ISBN
   9780878201860 (hardback) | ISBN 9780878201877 (ebook)
Subjects: LCGFT: Poetry.
Classification: LCC PJ5054.R49 A2 2020 (print) | LCC PJ5054.R49 (ebook) |
   DDC 892.41/6--dc23
LC record available at https://lccn.loc.gov/2019052364
LC ebook record available at https://lccn.loc.gov/2019052365
                                2013042361

Set in Arno Pro by Raphaël Freeman MISTD, Renana Typesetting
Cover design by Elena Barschazki
Photograph of Ruebner thanks to Mel Freilich

OLD MAN IN LOVE

The old man's in love, the old man loves!
His frozen body is all of a sudden ablaze.
A pine tree adorned with ivy he sees as a bird.
A bulging rock is for him a bull.
To the sand dunes he calls out, ho, how much water!
One, he claims, is two and none other.
At the midday sea he shouts Fire! Fire!
He's afraid, he dares, he dares, he's afraid.
Father, says he, father's a kid-goat,
and a kid-goat is *zuzei,* worthless coins of note.
To the stick he calls: Dog. A dog will chase.
And *shunrah*'s a cat or tiger or chimp out of place.
The Angel of Death will he kill or be killed?
Who is the slaughtering *shochet*? He asks, and how will
we live if no one dies?
Is he not sated? Does he still hunger?
The old man loves! He loves! He loves!

# CONTENTS

III / MORE NO MORE

# INTRODUCTION

In late 2013, Hebrew poet Tuvia Ruebner published his fifteenth poetry collection, which he titled *Last Ones*. In interviews and in personal communications following that publication, and following his ninetieth birthday a few months later (in January 2014), he declared that that poetry collection would, indeed, be his last one. The poems of that book felt to him both optimistic and summarizing, and – as he offered in a May 2014 newspaper interview marked by his characteristic whimsy – "...in the meantime, I don't want to ruin that for the reader. Also, after titling a collection *Last Ones*, it's a problem publishing another book – no?"[1]

But, the poet kept writing. In his ninety-first and ninety-second years in particular, Ruebner experienced a period of poetic productivity such as he had never previously known. "I write now almost every day," he described in the aforementioned interview, "...exactly like a good hen. Even if what I lay are not always golden eggs. This has never happened to me before. It's like a flood. Like a last flame."[2] Working in his small kibbutz home with its art-covered walls (Breughel's "Hunters in the Snow," Giacometti's "Walking Man," paintings by Vermeer, and much more), Ruebner composed, crafted, and revised poem after poem – as though he were a poet in the flush of first youthful creativity and not a poet in the tenth decade of his life. When visitors would come, Ruebner would pull out from beside the armchair where he sat the folder of new poems, in order to recite to the avid listening ears his latest creations. Before too long, it became apparent that there was a book to be published – and then another, and yet another.

And so, *Last Ones* was not last. In 2015 *The Crossroads*, and then in 2017 the collection titled *Still Before,* were published – the titles of both books subverting with gentle irony the poet's own earlier certainty of endings. In 2018, after months of composing haikus, Ruebner published *Seventeen*, a collection devoted in full to these seventeen-syllable poems, a form to which he had never devoted himself so fully. And in spring 2019, a few months after the poet's ninety-fifth birthday, Ruebner's nineteenth poetry collection, titled *More No More*, was published. *This* one, he said, would really be his last.[3]

1. "'By Chance I Stayed Alive': A Conversation with Tuvia Ruebner." Yoni Livneh. *Yediot Ahronot* Literature Section, 30.5.2014, 24–25 [Hebrew]. All translations from Hebrew are mine.
2. Ibid.
3. In April 2019, I sent this introduction and the completed manuscript of translations to Ruebner, so he could read and comment on them. A week later, I travelled to Kibbutz Merchavia to visit and review together with him his corrections. Our session began, as all our meetings

And so, the poetry collection *More No More* is his last. On July 29th 2019, at half past midnight, Tuvia Ruebner passed away. The last poem he composed in late June – a love poem titled "A Man Writes a Poem to his Wife on Her 87th Birthday" – had been published in the Friday newspaper ten days earlier.

There are few examples of such prolific, and consistently original and significant, artistic production by poets in their very old age. But the wonder of this poet's continued creativity seems even greater within the context of the many personal tragedies that marked his life, any one of which could have rendered him mute. Born in Slovakia in 1924, the seventeen-year-old Ruebner arrived in Palestine on his own in 1941, having left his entire family behind – a farewell that Ruebner described as "still weighing on his bones" many decades later.[4] Manfred and Elisabet Ruebner, Ruebner's parents, and his twelve-year-old little sister Alice, nicknamed Litzi, were murdered in Auschwitz in the summer of 1942, news the young Ruebner received only much later. The loss of his family, said Ruebner, was always before his eyes.[5] Settled in Kibbutz Merchavia in the Jezreel Valley, Ruebner married, and in early 1950 he and his young wife Ada – mother of his infant daughter Miriam – were involved in a bus accident. Ada was killed at once and Ruebner was seriously wounded. With burns over much of his body, Ruebner's recovery was slow and painful. Three years later, he married again, to Galila Jizreeli, a young pianist from Kibbutz Ein Harod, and two sons were born. The family flourished, and Ruebner taught and wrote, slowly establishing his literary reputation. However, yet another unimaginable tragedy lurked in the future: in 1983 Ruebner's younger son, Moran, then twenty-three years old, traveled to South America for an extended trip and after a period, disappeared. No trace of him was ever found.[6]

These lost beloveds wander also through Ruebner's late poetry, pain and sorrow undiminished by the decades that passed since their loss. There is, however, one shift in these poems: in some of them, the poem moves from "unrelenting longing," to the poet's imagining his own passing from the world – the only

did, with a small glass of whiskey. Ruebner offered corrections and clarifications, and gave his approval for this book. He was generous with praise and expressed his pleasure at having another English language collection being readied for publication. This paragraph's final sentence was then in the present tense ("This one, he says, will really be his last"), and led the poet to smile. The short paragraph that follows is now, with great sadness, added to the introduction.

4. From Ruebner's memoir *A Short Long Life*, 2006, 7 [Hebrew].

5. As a family photo taken shortly before Ruebner left Slovakia hangs above his desk, his lost family was literally ever before his eyes.

6. For a more extensive and comprehensive biographic and artistic overview of Ruebner, see "Introduction" in *In the Illuminated Dark*, 2015, xvii–xxviii. In addition, see "Chronology of Tuvia Ruebner," also in *Illuminated*, 343–45.

event, it seems, that can end his longing. Thus Ruebner writes in a tight and restrained six-line poem, one of the many about his lost son: "His eyes are in my eyes / His body is the body of a dream/…/ I will not let him go / Till I die" ("Untitled," p. 97). In another poem, the speaker seems to find relief in the poem's concluding realization: "If I join you, my lost ones / you will no longer be my lost ones. / Not a single one" ("Will," p. 101). The "lost ones" include, especially in these late collections , also the close friends and artist-colleagues who have passed away – a vibrant community of Israeli artists and poets, many of them immigrant/refugees like Ruebner himself, some of them survivors. There were those who died many years before (like the writers Dan Pagis and Yaakov Shabtai) and more recent losses (such as the artist Yosl Bergner). Ruebner bids them farewell one by one, even as he continues conversing with them. With the passing of Haim Gouri in early 2018, Ruebner became the last poet of his generation left.[7]

Poetry propelled by memories and informed by loss may be considered customary and expected from an old poet; what is less typical, perhaps, is poetry intimately engaged with the events of the day. And yet, in these late collections, even as the poet himself rarely leaves his home, Ruebner remains fully engaged in the world beyond the confines of his kibbutz room. Inevitably, it is the direction of Israel – the place that saved him, the land that promised redemption – that preoccupies and troubles him in particular. Everywhere he looks, the poet sees violence, racism, and corruption reigning supreme: "O how have you become / a land where truth turns its back on itself," the poet-prophet laments ("*Eikha* / O How," p. 113). Indeed, throughout these late collections, in language both bold and uncompromising, Ruebner offers fierce protest against the lies being told by those in power, against the crimes routinely committed in the preservation of power, and against the steady perversion of the Holocaust legacy.[8] Despite the toil and the toll of writing such poems, at any age, the poet keeps working and writing, resisting complacency and refusing the complicity of silence and despair.

And then there are the love poems: love poems to his beloved wife of six-ty-six years, love poems to the Jezreel valley landscapes he inhabited his entire adult life, love poems to the classical music that always nurtured his spirit, to

7. Gouri passed away on January 31st, 2018, at ninety-four years of age (coincidentally, the day after Ruebner's ninety-fourth birthday). For years, the two old poets were considered "Elders of the Tribe" – with Ruebner always pointing out that he was "much" younger than Gouri, by four months.

8. "I see the Holocaust as the *caesura* of human history," said Ruebner in the summer of 2014. "This 'phenomenon' [of the Holocaust] created a new man who should be wary of himself, for he's understood what he is capable of" (personal communication). The appropriation of the Holocaust legacy for fostering nationalistic fervor "demeans the dead," asserted Ruebner.

the birds that still sing and the dawn that still comes. "The old man's in love," writes Ruebner in the poem that stands as epigraph to this English collection, "the old man loves!" Life moves relentlessly, often violently, onward – and yet, the poet's creative imaginings can transform the world (as the poem's metaphors suggest), even as his musical iterations (in this instance, the poem's light-hearted rhyming couplets) seem to turn darkness into celebration. Thus, within the replenishing force of creativity and of loving so abundantly, the unsated poet – "still hungering" – lives on.

   Of course, death is also present in these late poems; for a nonagenarian poet, how could it be otherwise? Ruebner talks to death, wonders about it, how and when it will come. In one poem he wishes for himself a speedy passage from this world: "At the hour he rises up / to annihilate me – / Oh then, please, in one fell swoop, / not two, but one! // May it be done, / Amen" ("At the Hour," p. 103). In another, he asks – of whom, it isn't clear – that he may gently slip into death as into his signature white *galabiyah*, "or better yet: as in surfing the waves / to surf into the nothing" ("Don't," p. 131). As with his poems of protest and of love, these poems too are marked by the frankness of their gaze, and the honesty and fearlessness of their engagement. For the poet at the age of nine-ty-five, death was not an opponent, nor a force to refuse or struggle with; and yet, these poems offer a lingering sense of reluctance to pass out of this world. "Is this not the best of all worlds?" wonders the poet, confessing his desire "... to say / again and again, life is beautiful. It's beautiful to be alive" ("On the Longest Day of the Year," p. 109). Thus, one discovers in these late poems what has been present throughout Tuvia Ruebner's astonishing oeuvre but announces itself now, toward the end, with even greater force: this poet of unspeakable losses and unfathomable sorrows is no less a poet of praise. "I knew that the unsayable is / unsayable," the poet admits in a very late text. And still,

> I orbited around it
> like around a black hole
> in order to say in dark days
> there are moments of light, praise for life.[9]

In the tradition of Psalms, Ruebner's late poems marvel at the breath given, at the day offered, and at the wonder of a word speaking from the page – even as the poet himself gently moved toward silence.[10]

---

9.  "I Am Still," p. 127.
10.  See the last line of the last poem of Ruebner's last book, "Silence for you is praise" ("Words," p. 155).

# A NOTE ON ORGANIZATION

This book is dedicated to poems Ruebner wrote and published from 2014–2019 (from his ninetieth to his ninety-fifth years). I have chosen poems from three of the four collections published in these years: *The Crossroads* (2015), *Still Before* (2017) and *More No More* (2019).[11] The selection process regarding which poems to include from each book was governed by various attributes and considerations, from a poem's representativeness or singularity, to a poem's beauty. As is self-evident, my personal preferences and aesthetic judgments influenced the selection. The poems from each book appear in their own section. In determining the placement of the poems within each section, I have adhered to the order in which they appear in the original collections. Ruebner, together with his editors Rafi Weichert (*The Crossroads*) and Liat Kaplan (*Still Before* and *More No More*), invested in each book's trajectory considerable thought and meaning; though I've included only a portion of each book's poems, I believe that the original trajectories of Ruebner's collections are still represented here.

The book's endnotes serve several purposes. First, the notes elucidate the many biblical, liturgical and talmudic allusions woven through Ruebner's texts by directing the reader toward relevant source materials. The second purpose of the notes is to provide historical and biographic information that impacts one's understanding of the poem. Finally, any pronounced deviation from the Hebrew original, from alternative enjambments and change in stanza length to lexis changes, are addressed and explained in the notes.

Finally, a note on Ruebner's untitled poems: in the Table of Contents, these untitled poems are identified by the poem's first line in brackets. However, the poems themselves are marked only by the asterisk at page's top, in order to recreate the opening spatial silence evoked by an absent title and in adherence to Ruebner's own presentation of these texts.

11. But for the few haiku poems Ruebner published in *Still Before*, I have not included in this collection Ruebner's poems from his haiku collection, *Seventeen*. As the poems of that collection are singularly defined by their strict syllabic form, translating them with adherence to that form (as one must) renders English versions that are stilted and do not adequately stand on their own as poetic entities.

# I

# THE CROSSROADS

# הַיְדְן

הַיְדְן הַהוֹלֵךְ וּמַזְקִין.
מָה יָדַע כַּאֲשֶׁר כָּתַב אֶת הַפֶּרֶק הַשֵּׁנִי
שֶׁל רְבִיעִיַּת הַמֵּיתָרִים, אוֹפּוּס 77, מס' 1?
הַאִם חָשַׁשׁ מִפְּנֵי מַה שֶּׁחָשׁ?
הַאִם חָשׁ שֶׁמַּשֶּׁהוּ עָתִיד לִקְרוֹת?
מַשֶּׁהוּ אָפֵל, מַשֶּׁהוּ נוֹרָא שֶׁאֵין לְהַבִּיעַ
לֹא בְּמִלִּים וְלֹא בִּצְלִילִים?
מִמָּה הָיָה לוֹ לַחֲשֹׁשׁ? בָּטוּחַ בְּבֵיתוֹ בְּשֶׁנְבְּרוּן,
"בְּרִיאַת הָעוֹלָם" מֻשְׁלֶמֶת, וְהוּא חֲבִיב הַקֵּיסָר.
מִפְּלִישַׁת הַבַּרְבָּרִים לְוִינָה שֶׁלּוֹ, לְבוּרְגֶנְלַנְד,
שִׁלְטוֹן הַבַּרְבָּרִים בְּכָל מָקוֹם?
תְּבוּנָה תְּלוּיַת תּוֹעֵבָה?

לֹא צָרִיךְ לְהַלֵּךְ בְּדִמְיוֹנוֹת,
לְהַמְצִיא אֶפְשָׁרֻיּוֹת דִּמְיוֹנִיּוֹת
בְּיַחַס לְאָמָּנִים וּלְאָמָּנוּת.
אֲנָשִׁים כָּמוֹנִי, פַּרְטִיטוּרוֹת לָהֶם שֶׁטַח מְכַסֶּה לִכְלוּךְ זְבוּבִים.
לָכֵן אֲנִי שָׁם תַּקְלִיטוֹר וּמַקְשִׁיב.
אֲוִיר הַבֹּקֶר עוֹדוֹ קָרִיר.

שׁוּם זִכְרוֹנוֹת.
הַפֶּרֶסְטוֹ סוֹחֵף.
הָעוּרְבָּן מְנַסֶּה לְחַקּוֹת אוֹתוֹ עַל פִּי דַּרְכּוֹ
וְהָעֶפְרוֹנִי עַל פִּי דַּרְכּוֹ שֶׁלּוֹ.
הָעוֹלָם מַחֲזִיק, אֵינוֹ מִתְפּוֹרֵר
וּבוֹ, בַּסּוֹבֵב הַזָּקֵן הַזֶּה, עַל צִירוֹ הֶהָזוּי שְׁוֵה-נֶפֶשׁ
עִם שׂוֹחֲטָיו וְלֵיצָנָיו, עִם חֲכָמָיו וּרְשָׁעָיו,
עִם שׁוֹדְדֵי עֲנָיָיו, וְעִם תַּמָּיו
הַמְצִיא הַיְדְן אֶת רְבִיעִיַּת הַמֵּיתָרִים.
דְּבָרִים פְּלָאִים קוֹרִים. תַּעֲנוּג לִחְיוֹת.

# HAYDN

Haydn, growing old.
What did he know when he wrote the second movement
of the String Quartets, Opus 77, number 1?
Did he fear what he was sensing?
Did he sense what was soon to happen?
Something dark, something terrible not to be told
not in words and not in musical notes?
What did he have to fear? Safe in his house in Schönbrunn,
"The Creation" perfect, and he a favorite of the Kaiser.
Fear of the barbarians invading his Vienna, his Burgenland,
reign of the barbarians everywhere?
Reason subservient to abomination?

One needs no flight of fancy
to invent imaginary possibilities
regarding artists and art.
For people like me a musical score seems a surface covered in flyspecks.
That's why I put on a record and listen.
The morning air is still cool.
No memories.
The presto is stirring.
The jaybird tries to imitate it in its way
and the lark in its own way.
The world goes on, without crumbling
and on it, on this old planet spinning round on its delusional indifferent axis,
with its killers and its clowns, its wise and its wicked,
with the plunderers of its poor, and with its innocent,
Haydn created the String Quartets.
Wondrous things happen. What a joy to be alive.

שִׁפְעַת פרחים
לבתי, למרים


שִׁפְעַת פְּרָחִים.
פִּרְחֵי הַנֶּפֶשׁ בְּכָל הַגְּוָנִים,
כָּל־כָּךְ
הַרְבֵּה
חַיִּים.
אֵיךְ הִיא הָעֵצָה
הַנֶּפֶשׁ, אֵיךְ הָעֵצָה
כָּכָה לִפְרֹחַ?

כָּל דִּבּוּר כּוֹרֵעַ בֶּרֶךְ לְעֻמַּת הַיֹּפִי הַזֶּה.
שׁוּם לָשׁוֹן לֹא תַּשִּׂיג טַעַם צֶבַע.
כָּל הַמִּלִּים רַק תּוֹתָבוֹת.

דָּם וּשְׁכַח
אֵיךְ תִּעְתְּעוּ בָּךְ עֵינֶיךָ
לִרְאוֹת בְּמִקְבָּצִים קְטַנִּים שֶׁל אֲדַמְדַּם,
כָּתֹם, אַרְגָּמָן, כָּחֹל, צָהֹב, יָרֹק, סָגֹל, לָבָן
בְּהִירִים וּמְעֻרְפָּלִים, זוֹהֲרִים וְכֵהִים
אֶת חַיֵּי נַפְשְׁךָ כְּשִׁפְעַת פְּרָחִים.

שִׁפְעַת פְּרָחִים, שִׁפְעַת פְּרָחִים.


4

## A PLENITUDE OF FLOWERS

*for my daughter, for Miriam*


A plenitude of flowers.
The soul's flowers in every hue,
so much
plentiful
life.
How has she dared,
the soul, how has she dared
thus to bloom?

All speech bends its knee before this beauty.
No language can achieve the taste of color.
All words are only substitutes.

Be silent and forget
how your eyes deceived you
into seeing in small patches of blush red,
orange, indigo, blue, yellow, green, violet, white
light and cloudy, gleaming and dark
your soul's life as a plenitude of flowers.

Plenitude of flowers, a plenitude of flowers.

כתיבת שירים

כְּתִיבַת שִׁירִים בְּגִיל תִּשְׁעִים – עָמָל.
הַגּוּף מַכְבִּיד וְהָעֵינַיִם טְרוּטוֹת,
כֹּחַ הַהַמְצָאָה מִצָּה אֶת עַצְמוֹ,
הַמַּחֲשָׁבוֹת לְאַט־לְאַט־לְאַט, הָרֶגֶשׁ
רָדוּם מְעַט.

אַךְ מִי אָמַר לִי: כְּתֹב!
אֲנִי? הֲלֹא? הָאִי־אֶפְשָׁר־שֶׁלֹּא,
כִּי בַּמִּלִים אֲנִי נוֹלָד?

כְּתַרְגִּילֵי פְּסַנְתְּרָן יוֹם יוֹם
אֲנִי מַשְׁחִיר אֶת לְבֶן הַנְּיָר בְּסִימָנִים,
בְּבוֹא הַיּוֹם אוּלַי יָעִידוּ כִּי הָיִיתִי וּבַשִּׁיר
עוֹדֶנִּי כָּאן כְּמִי אֲשֶׁר בִּקֵּשׁ

לְהַלֵּל וּלְהוֹדוֹת עַל הַקַּיָּם,
עַל הַטָּנְדוּ שֶׁבּוֹ
שֶׁל הַשְּׁלִילָה וְהַחִיּוּב, שֶׁל הַטָּמִיר וְהַגָּלוּי,
שֶׁל הַנִּתָּן וְהַנִּמְנָע

וְעַל הַלֹא־קַיָּם שֶׁרַק תַּזְכִּיר אוֹתוֹ
וּכְבָר הֶחֱטֵאתָ,
מִלָּה אַחַת –
תְּנוּעַת אֲוִיר חָלְפָה.

# WRITING POEMS

Writing poems at the age of ninety – hard work.
The body is a burden and the eyes are bleary,
the powers of imagination have exhausted themselves,
thoughts move slowly slowly slowly, the heart
is a little drowsy.

So who told me: Write!
Me? Really? Is it the impossible-not-to,
for in words I am born?

Like daily piano practice
I blacken the page's whiteness with marks,
one day maybe they'll testify that I existed and in the poem
am still here as he who wanted

to praise and give thanks for what is,
for existence's dyad
of negation and affirmation, of the hidden and the revealed,
of the given and the withheld

and for the non-existent that in just mentioning it
you've already missed the mark,
one word –
a flutter of air passed by.

הדרך

לבני, לעידן


הַדֶּרֶךְ
הַדֶּרֶךְ הַזֹּאת
מִכָּאן
עַד
שָׁם
רַק הַדֶּרֶךְ הַזֹּאת
צְעַד
צְעַד
הַבָּתִּים נָשְׁרוּ
הָעֵצִים נִשְׂאוּ בָּרוּחַ
לֹא שֶׁמֶשׁ
לֹא צֵל
רַק הַדֶּרֶךְ הַזֹּאת
צְעַד
צְעַד
הַדֶּרֶךְ
רַק הַדֶּרֶךְ
רַק הַדֶּרֶךְ הַזֹּאת

## THE PATH

*for my son, for Idan*

The path

this path

from here

to

there

just this path

step

by step

the houses dropped away

the trees were carried off by winds

not sun

not shade

just this path

step

by step

the path

just the path

just this path

רק נוכל נותן יותר ממה שיש לו

כִּמְעַט כָּל יוֹם כָּעֵת בְּתִשְׁעִים מַטְבִּילָה הַשִּׁירָה
בֵּיצָה בְּקִנִּי, לֹא תָּמִיד בֵּיצַת זָהָב.
אַךְ רַק חָכָם־בִּפְרוּטָה יַחְשֹׁב זָהָב לְסַם־חַיִּים.
גַּם סֵבֶל מְבַקֵּשׁ אֶת רְשׁוּת־הַדִּבּוּר, גַּם זַעַם, אַכְזָבָה,
חֲרָטָה, מֶחְדָּל.
פָּנִים רַבּוֹת לַחַיִּים, הֲפֹךְ בָּן וַהֲפֹךְ בָּן –
כֻּלָּן יָפוֹת לַשִּׁירָה. גַּם הַמְּרִירוּת שֶׁל כִּשָּׁלוֹן –
רוֹצִים לִטְעֹם?

## ONLY A CROOK GIVES MORE THAN HE HAS

Almost every day now at ninety, poetry lays
another egg in my nest, not always a golden egg.
But only the penny-wise would think gold the elixir of life.
Suffering also asks to speak, as does rage, disappointment too,
ruin, regret.
So many facets to life, turn them over and over again –
all are beautiful to poetry. Even the bitterness of failure –
do you want to taste?

הַיּוֹם נִפְרַדְתִּי מִדָּן, מֵעֹזֶר, מִיַּעֲנְקֵלֶה.
הֵם מֵתוּ אֶצְלִי מָוֶת שֵׁנִי.
מֹשֶׁה, אִישׁ גְּנָזִים, גָּנַז אוֹתָם וְצָרָרַם.
לָעַד נֶעֱלָם מִמֶּנִּי כְּתַב־יָדָם הַחַי וְכָל מַה
שֶּׁאָמְרוּ לִי וְלֹא אָמְרוּ בְּאִגְּרוֹתֵיהֶם וּבַגְּלוּיוֹת.
וְאַף־עַל־פִּי־כֵן, כְּעוֹף הַחוֹל קָמוּ לְעֵינַי בְּגוּפָם הַבָּהִיר,
"כִּי אֵין קָרוֹב לְלִבְּךָ כְּזֶה שֶׁאָבַד" כָּתוּב בְּ"אַחֲרוֹנִים,"
וַהֲרֵי גַּם אַחֲרוֹנִים אֵינָם אַחֲרוֹנִים
וְאִם הַגֶּשֶׁם מָנַע אֶת עַצְמוֹ מִבּוֹא בַּחֹרֶף הַזֶּה –
הִנֵּה, הַכַּלָּנִיּוֹת מַאְדִּימוֹת וְהַתִּרְמוֹס מַכְחִיל בַּגִּנָּה
וְהַשָּׂדוֹת מְלֵאִים חַרְדָּל־בָּר רַקָּפוֹת וְנַרְקִיסִים הֵם נִיחוֹחַ
וְהָעֵשֶׂב גָּדֵל וְצוֹבֵעַ אֶת עֵינֵינוּ.
פֶּתִי מַאֲמִין לְכָל דָּבָר, אָמְרָה לִי הָאָחוֹת אֱמוּנָה,
אֲהוּבַת נַפְשִׁי אֶת שָׁכַבְתִּי חֲצִי שָׂרוּף.
הַאִם אֲנִי אַךְ מְדַמֶּה לִכְתֹּב מֵעֵין שִׁיר פְּרִידָה?
וַהֲלֹא בַּחֲלוֹם הַלַּיְלָה אַתֶּם אִתִּי,
דְּמוּתְכֶם מְאִירָה אֶת פְּנֵי עַפְעַפַּי, אֲבוּדַי.

23.2.2014

Today I bid farewell to Dan, to Ozer, to Yankele.
They died for me a second death.
Moshe, the archivist, packed them up and filed them away.
Their living handwriting is forever hidden from me with all
they said to me and didn't say in their letters and postcards.
And still, like the Phoenix, they rose before my eyes in their bright body,
"For nothing is closer to your heart than what has been lost," as is written in
    Last Ones,
after all even last ones aren't last
and if the rain has stopped itself from falling this winter –
still, the anemones are reddening, the lupines are turning blue in the garden
and the fields are full of wild mustard seed, cyclamens, the narcissus are
    fragrant
and the grass is growing and coloring our eyes.
A fool believes everything, the nurse Emunah told me,
she who was my heart's beloved while I lay half-burnt.
Am I trying to write a type of farewell poem?
But in the night's dream you are all with me,
your images shine light inside my closed eyes, you, my lost ones.

שׁוּב אביב

שׁוּב אָבִיב
שׁוּב לְהִתְעוֹרֵר
שׁוּב אָמוּר
לְהִתְעוֹרֵר
הוֹ, כֵּן
וַעֲבָרִי מַפִּיל אוֹתִי
בֵּין פְּרָחִים, כֵּן
פְּרָחִים, וְרַגְלוֹ
עַל צַוָּארִי.

# AGAIN IT'S SPRING

Again it's spring
again to wake up
again supposed
to wake up
oh, yes
and my past drops me
among flowers, yes
flowers, and its foot
on my neck.

*

הַשְּׁתִיקָה
אַחֲרֵי הַיְקִיצָה

הַשְּׁתִיקָה
אַחֲרֵי הַדִּבּוּר

אַחֲרֵי הַקּוֹל

שְׁתִיקַת הַחֶדֶר, הַסְּפָרִים

הַשְּׁתִיקָה
אַחֲרֵי טִפָּה נוֹשֶׁרֶת

הַשְּׁתִיקָה
אַחֲרֵי הַצִּלְצוּל בַּדֶּלֶת

הַשְּׁתִיקָה
שֶׁל אַף־אֶחָד

שֶׁל הַשָּׁמַיִם הַתְּלוּיִים כִּסְמַרְטוּטִים

הַשְּׁתִיקָה
אַחֲרֵי שְׁרִיקַת הַנֵּץ

אַחֲרֵי הַיְבָבָה

שְׁתִיקַת הַחוֹל הַנּוֹדֵד לְאִטּוֹ
עַל פְּנֵי הַשֶּׁטַח הָרֵיק.

*

The silence
After awakening

The silence
After speaking

After the voice

The silence of the room, the books

The silence
After a drop falls away

The silence
After the ringing at the door

The silence
Of no one

Of the skies dangling like rags

The silence
After the hawk's screech

After the weeping

The silence of the sand slowly wandering
Over the empty space.

כמעט אחי

ד.פ.

אָמוּר הָיִיתִי לְהַסְפִּידְךָ בְּפָמְבֵּי, בְּבֵית הַהַלְוָיוֹת שָׁם בְּסַנְהֶדְרִיָּה.
הַמִּלִּים סֵרְבוּ, הָפְכוּ עַצְמָן לְמִלְמוּל חֲסַר פֵּשֶׁר.
הָיִיתָ שׂוֹנֵא הֶסְפֵּד כָּזֶה.

כְּשֶׁרְאִיתִיךָ בְּלִי לִרְאוֹת מִתַּחַת הַטַּלִּית, מִין מַשֶּׁהוּ,
עָמוּד שֶׁדַּרְתִּי הִתְכּוֹפֵף בְּכִמְעַט תִּשְׁעִים מַעֲלוֹת, כְּמוֹ אֵצֶל
זִקְנֵי הַכְּפָרִים בַּקַּרְפָּטִים, כְּמוֹ שֶׁנִּבְּאוּ רוֹפְאֶיךָ אֶת עֲתִידְךָ וְטָעוּ.

אֵיזֶה כְּעוּר הַפֶּה בְּאֵין שִׁנַּיִם שֶׁבָּלַע אוֹתְךָ. לוּ שָׁאֲלוּ אוֹתְךָ,
קָשֶׁה לִי לְהַאֲמִין שֶׁלֹּא הָיִיתָ מְסָרֵב לְטֶקֶס זֶה, כָּל-כָּךְ בְּלִי דִּיגְנִיטִי.
וְאוּלַי כְּלָל לֹא הִרְגַּשְׁתָּ, אַף פַּעַם לֹא בָּטוּחַ אִם אַתָּה חַי בֶּאֱמֶת?

כְּשֶׁבִּקַּרְתִּי אֶצְלְךָ בַּ"הֲדַסָּה" וּכְבָר יָדַעְתָּ, יָשַׁבְתָּ לְיַד מִטָּתְךָ
לֹא בִּלְבוּשׁ בֵּית-הַחוֹלִים אֶלָּא בְּפִיגָ'מָה מִבֵּיתְךָ מְגֹהֶצֶת לְמִשְׁעִי
לְקַבֵּל אֶת פְּנֵי הָרוֹפְאִים בְּבִקּוּר הַבֹּקֶר.

סִפַּרְתָּ לִי אֶת חֲלוֹמְךָ בְּאוֹתוֹ לַיְלָה: "שִׁנֵּינוּ בְּמִין רַכֶּבֶת
מִכְנַס סְפָרוּתִי שֶׁשָּׁעָמֵם עַד מָוֶת.
אֲנִי יוֹצֵא בַּתַּחֲנָה הַזֹּאת, אַתָּה בְּעוֹד שְׁתֵּי תַּחֲנוֹת."

מֵאָז הִגִּיעֲךָ אַרְצָה, לְמֶרְחַבְיָה, הָיִינוּ חֲבוּקִים. כִּמְעַט אַחִים.
אֲבָל אַתָּה, בְּשֵׁשׁ שָׁנִים צָעִיר, גָּדוֹל הָיִיתָ מִמֶּנִּי כִּמְעַט בַּכֹּל.
תָּמִיד הִקְדַּמְתָּ אוֹתִי. גַּם עַכְשָׁו.

18

# ALMOST MY BROTHER

*D.P.*


I was supposed to eulogize you publicly, there at the funeral home in
    Sanhedria
But the words refused, turned themselves into meaningless mutterings.
You would have hated such a eulogy.

When I saw you without seeing you there under the *tallit*, some something,
my back bent forward to almost ninety degrees, like the old men of a
Carpathian village, as your doctors said would happen to you and they were
    wrong.

How ugly the toothless mouth that swallowed you. If you had been asked,
I find it hard to believe you wouldn't have refused such a rite, so without
    dignity.
And perhaps you felt nothing, as you were never certain you were really alive?

When I visited you at Hadassah Hospital and you already knew, you sat
    beside your bed
not in hospital gown but in pajamas, brought from home and perfectly
    ironed,
to receive the doctors on their morning rounds.

You told me your dream of that same night: "We are both on some kind of
    train
returning from a literary conference that had bored us to death.
I get off at this station, you in two more."

Since you first arrived in this land, to Merchavia, we were intertwined.
    Almost brothers.
But you, six years my junior, were senior to me in almost everything.
You always preceded me. Now too.

עֶשְׂרִים וְשֶׁבַע שָׁנִים בִּלְעָדֶיךָ. לֹא, לֹא בִּלְעָדֶיךָ, הֲרֵי מְשׂוֹחֲחִים.
כְּמוֹ מְחִיאַת־כַּף בְּיָד אַחַת, שִׂיחָה בְּקוֹל אֶחָד. זֶה אֶפְשָׁרִי?
נִרְאֶה שֶׁכֵּן בְּשָׁמְעִי: שׁוּרָה זֹאת מְיֻתֶּרֶת, יוֹתֵר מִדַּי מִלִּים.

Twenty-seven years without you. No, not without you, after all we're talking
  now.
Like one hand clapping, a conversation with one voice. Is that even possible?
It seems so, as I now hear: "That line is unnecessary, too many words."

מה אפשר לומר למתים

לזכר עדה


שׁוּבִי, אָנָּא, שׁוּבִי, לַמְרוֹת הַכֹּל!
נַצְחִי אוֹתוֹ וְשׁוּבִי, תְּנִי מִלִּים.
אֲנִי עָיֵף. אֵינִי מֵבִין דָּבָר.
הַכֹּל הָפוּךְ.
אִלֵּם כָּל־כָּךְ, הַכֹּל אִלֵּם כָּל־כָּךְ.

אֵיךְ אֶנְשֹׁם בִּלְעָדַיִךְ? בְּלִי רֵיחַ עוֹרֵךְ,
בְּלִי צְחוֹקֵךְ, אֵיךְ?

הֲרֵי אֲנִי יוֹדֵעַ, אַךְ בּוֹאִי, שׁוּבִי
וְהִפְכִי שׁוּב אֶת הַחֶדֶר
רָאוּי לָגוּר בּוֹ וְאָבִין אֶת הַשֻּׁלְחָן
שֶׁהוּא שֻׁלְחָן וְהַכִּסֵּא שֶׁהוּא כִּסֵּא.
הָרֵיקוּת הַזֹּאת, הָרֵיקוּת הַנּוֹרָאָה הַזֹּאת.

אֵין לִי דְּמָעוֹת, אֲבָל הַאִם יוֹם הוּא בַּעֲלוֹת הַשֶּׁמֶשׁ
וָעֶרֶב בְּבוֹאָהּ?
וְאֵיךְ אֶגְלֹשׁ לְאֹרֶךְ יְרֵכַיִךְ וְאֵיךְ אָשִׂים רֹאשִׁי
בַּשֶּׁקַע בֵּין שָׁדַיִךְ וְאֵיךְ אֶצְבְּעוֹתַי יַחֲלִיקוּ עַל שְׂעָרֵךְ
כְּמוֹ הָרוּחַ עַל אַדְוַת הַיָּם?

אוֹבִיל אוֹתָךְ לְאֹרֶךְ חֹרֶשׁ הַזֵּיתִים,
לוּ רַק יָכֹלְתִּי שׁוּב לָרִיב אִתָּךְ רִיב קַל,
נִכְנָע לָךְ בִּרְצוֹן.

קָנִינוּ לָנוּ שְׁבוּת בַּשֶּׁקֶר.
קַלֵּי קַלּוּת גּוֹלְשִׁים לְמַלְבּוּשׁוֹ
אַף שֶׁהוּא דַּק מִדַּי.
נֹאמַר "יִמְתְּקוּ לָךְ הָרְגָבִים"
וְ"לֹא נִשְׁכָּחֵךְ לְעוֹלָם." מַה זֶּה?
מַה כָּל זֶּה?

# WHAT CAN WE SAY TO THE DEAD

*In memory of Ada*


Come back, please, come back, in spite of everything!
Vanquish it and come back, give me words.
I'm tired. I don't understand a thing.
Everything is upside down.
So mute, all is so very mute.

How will I breathe without you? Without the scent of your skin,
without your laughter, how?

Of course I know, still, come, come back
and make this room again
worthy to live in and I'll understand the table
is a table and the chair is a chair.
This emptiness, this terrible emptiness.

I have no tears, but is it day when the sun rises
and evening when it sets?
And how will I slide down the length of your thighs, how will I place my head
in the hollow between your breasts and how will my fingers glide over your hair
like the wind over the sea's ripples?

I'll lead you along the olive grove,
if only I could argue with you, again, one small quarrel,
yielding to you happily.

We acquire our rest with a lie.
We slip into its attire so easily
though it's too thin.
We say "May you rest in peace"
and "We'll never forget you." What is that?
What is all that?

בְּ־12 לְפֶבְּרוּאָר 1950
נִשְׂרַפְתְּ בְּבוּס בּוֹעֵר שָׁכוּב עַל צִדּוֹ
שֶׁמִּתּוֹכוֹ אוֹתִי גָּרְרוּ, כָּךְ סִפְּרוּ,
וְאוֹתָךְ לֹא. נִסִּיתִי שׁוּב לְהִכָּנֵס, סִפְּרוּ,
וּלְהוֹצִיא אוֹתָךְ, וְלֹא נָתְנוּ.
רָצִיתִי לְהִתְגַּלְגֵּל בִּשְׁלוּלִית, וְלֹא נָתְנוּ.
סִפְּרוּ לִי כִּי זֹהוּ אוֹתָךְ לְפִי טְבִיעַת שִׁנַּיִךְ.

נִסִּיתִי לְשַׁחֲזֵר הַיּוֹם מַה שֶׁכָּתַבְתִּי
שָׁנָה אַחֲרֵי מוֹתֵךְ.
אַךְ מָה אֶפְשָׁר לוֹמַר לַמֵּתִים?

On the 12th of February 1950

you were burned in a bus in flames lying on its side

from which they dragged me, so they said,

and not you. I tried to go back in, they said,

and pull you out, but they didn't let me.

I wanted to roll in a puddle, and they didn't let me.

They told me they identified you from your teeth.

I tried today to recreate what I wrote
one year after your death.
But what can we say to the dead?

# לפני דמדומי בוקר

לִפְנֵי דִמְדּוּמֵי בֹּקֶר רִאשׁוֹנִים מִסְתַּמֶּנֶת מֵעֵין בְּהִירוּת בָּאֲוִיר
כְּמוֹ כְּנַף הַמַּלְאָךְ שֶׁלַּסַּהַר הַדַּק מִן הַדַּק. הַפְּלָיָדִים שָׁקְעוּ.
אֲנִי שׁוֹכֵב וּבְעַלְוַת הָעֵצִים מְגַשֶּׁשֶׁת הָאַהֲבָה הַגְּדוֹלָה
כְּהֶמְיָה כִּמְעַט לֹא נִכֶּרֶת, הִיא סוֹבֶבֶת אֶת הַבַּיִת, אֲנִי חָשׁ.
הָאַהֲבָה הַגְּדוֹלָה שׁוֹאֶלֶת: אַיֶּכָּה? אֲנִי מֵשִׁיב: הִנֶּנִּי.
מַה תַּעֲשֶׂה הָאַהֲבָה הַגְּדוֹלָה בְּאוֹר הַיּוֹם הַמָּלֵא? מָה אֶעֱשֶׂה אֲנִי?
יֵשׁ כְּסוּפִים כְּמוֹ מַיִם אִלְּמִים שֶׁמְּחוֹלְלִים אֶת הָאֶבֶן.

## BEFORE FIRST MORNING TWILIGHT

Before first morning twilight some brightness in the air appears
like the angel wing of the thinner-than-thin Crescent. The Pleiades have set.
I'm lying down and in the treetops the Great Love is feeling her way
like a nearly unnoticed murmur, she circles the house, I sense her.
The Great Love asks: Where art thou? I answer: Here am I.
What will the Great Love do in the bright light of day? What will I do?
There are longings like mute waters that pierce the stone.

לילה

הִתְעוֹרַרְתִּי.
הוּא קוֹפֵץ עָלַי.
כְּמוֹ נָמֵר הַמִּדְבָּר הוּא קוֹפֵץ עָלַי.
לֹא נָמֵר רָעֵב, נָמֵר רַע לֵב.
בְּאֶמְצַע הַלַּיְלָה הוּא קוֹפֵץ עָלַי.
אֲנִי רוֹצָה לָשׁוּב וּלְהֵרָדֵם,
אֲנִי מְנַסָּה לִישֹׁן, מְנַסָּה, מְנַסָּה,
הַמֹּחַ עֵר וְלֹא נוֹתֵן.
נָמֵר מֹחִי טָרַף אֶת שְׁנָתִי
וְהִיא נוֹדֶדֶת מִגֶּדֶם מַחֲשָׁבָה
לְמַחֲשָׁבָה קְטוּעָה
בְּמִדְבַּר הַלַּיְלָה הָרֵיק מֵרֹגַע.

# NIGHT

I awoke.

He pounces on me.

Like a desert leopard he pounces on me.

Not a hungry leopard, but a mean-hearted one.

In the middle of the night he pounces on me.

I want to fall back to sleep,

I try to sleep, I try and I try.

The mind is awake and won't allow it.

My mind's leopard has preyed upon my sleep

and it wanders from thought-stump

to thought-severed

in the night's desert that is empty of peace.

למפדוזה: טֶרָה פִֿרְמָה

סוּדָנִים, אֶרִיתְרֵאִים, אִישׁ וְאִשָּׁה, גַּם יְלָדִים.
הַיָּם לָבַשׁ לַיְלָה וְסוּסָיו הַשְּׁחֹרִים
דּוֹרְסִים, רוֹמְסִים אֶת רָאשֵׁי הַחוֹתְרִים,
הַקּוֹפְצִים מֵהָרַפְסוֹדָה הַגְּדוֹשָׁה
בִּתְשׁוּקָתָם שֶׁאֵינָהּ יוֹדַעַת גְּבוּל לָבוֹא
לְחוֹף מִבְטַחִים.

בַּחוֹל הָאָפֹר-כֵּהֶה – טֶרָה פִֿרְמָה
הִנֵּה הֵם מֻטָּלִים, גּוּפוֹת שֶׁל בָּבוֹת נְפוּחוֹת
עֵינַיִם יוֹצְאוֹת מֵאַרְבּוֹתֵיהֶן לְבָנוֹת, רַק הֵן
מְאִירוֹת בַּחֹשֶׁךְ סָבִיב.

בַּבֹּקֶר לִפְנֵי רַחְצַת הַתַּיָּרִים
יָבוֹאוּ מֵאַבְנֵי הַלֵּב
יִדְאֲגוּ לְסִלּוּק הַלֹּא-רְצוּיִים.
הַתַּיָּרִים לֹא יִרְאוּ, אִישׁ לֹא יִרְאֶה
הַמָּוֶת יַפְנֶה אֶת רֹאשׁוֹ מִבּוּשָׁה.

* טרה פֶרְמָה = יבשה סגורה; טרה פִרְמָה = אדמה מוצקה, יבשה.

---

30

# LAMPEDUSA: TERRA FERMÉ

Sudanese, Eritrean, man and woman, children too.
The sea dressed in night and its black horses
stomp and trample the heads of the rowers
who jump from the overflowing raft
in their borderless desire to reach
safe shores.

On the dark grey sands – *terra firma*
here they are strewn, swollen puppet bodies
eyes bulging from their white orbs, they alone
shine in the surrounding darkness.

By morning, before the tourists come to bathe,
the stone-hearted will come
to sweep the unwanted away.
The tourists will not see, no one will see
Death will look away in shame.

* Terra Fermé = closed land; Terra Firma = firm land, dry.

לְהִתְעוֹרֵר כָּל בֹּקֶר חַי – הַפְתָּעָה.

הַקּוֹרוֹת וְנַפְתּוּלֵיהֶן – הַפְתָּעָה עַל גַּב הַפְתָּעָה, אוֹ הָפוּךְ עַל הָפוּךְ.

חֲבֵרִים נֶעֱלָמִים – כְּבָר לֹא הַפְתָּעָה.

וְאִם בֶּאֱמֶת הַמַּמָּשׁוּת אֵינֶנָּה אֶלָּא מַעֲשֵׂה רְמִיָּה, כְּפִי שֶׁקָּרָאתִי,

הֲרֵי אֵין הַפְתָּעוֹת כְּלָל וּכְלָל.

וְאַף־עַל־פִּי־כֵן הֻפְתַּעְתִּי, הֻפְתַּעְתִּי מְאֹד כְּשֶׁלְּפֶתַע יָשַׁב עַל־יָדִי

יֶלֶד־שֶׁלֹּא־יֶלֶד אֶלָּא נַעַר־שֶׁלֹּא־נַעַר אֶלָּא אִישׁ צָעִיר שֶׁמֵּעוֹלָם

לֹא רָאִיתִי.

מִנַּיִן הוּא צָץ? הַאִם הָרוּחַ הִלְבִּישָׁה, הִפְשִׁיטָה, וְשׁוּב הִלְבִּישָׁה אוֹתוֹ

דְּמוּת? לֹא גְּבַהּ־קוֹמָה, יָדָיו גַּלְמָנִיּוֹת וְזָרִיזוֹת כְּאַחַת,

זְקָנוֹ שָׁחֹר וְכָךְ גַּם שְׂעַר רֹאשׁוֹ הַמְּקֻרְזָל, דִּבּוּרוֹ שָׁקֵט

כְּשֶׁל בַּעַל נִימוּסִין וְעֵינָיו גְּדוֹלוֹת כְּמוֹ אֵלּוּ שֶׁל קְדוֹשִׁים אֶתְיוֹפִּיִּים

בַּצִּיּוּרִים הָעַתִּיקִים, שֶׁסֵּבֶל כְּחָתָן וְשִׂמְחָה כְּכַלָּה הִתְמַזְּגוּ בָּהֶן.

נִשְׁמָתוֹ, אֲנִי חָשׁ, חִיּוּךְ.

הַפְתָּעָה, הַפְתָּעָה. הַפְתָּעָה כְּמוֹ שֶׁמֶשׁ חֲצוֹת בְּעֵמֶק יִזְרְעֶאל.

כָּתוּב: בַּמֻּפְלָא מִמְּךָ אַל תִּדְרֹשׁ. אֵינִי שׁוֹאֵל דָּבָר.

חֲלוֹמִי, בֵּיתִי בֵּיתְךָ, אַל תַּעַזְבֵנִי, אֲנִי חָסֵר בִּלְעָדֶיךָ.

## SURPRISES

To wake up every morning – a surprise.

History and its twistings – surprise atop surprise, or the other way around.

Friends disappearing – no longer a surprise.

And if reality is really nothing but a fraud, as I've read,

then there are no surprises at all.

And still, I was surprised, very surprised, when suddenly he sat down beside
me

a boy-who's-not-a-boy but a teen-who's-not-a-teen but a young man whom

I've never seen before.

From where did he appear? Did the wind dress him, strip him, then dress
him again

in human form? Not tall, his hands both clumsy and agile,

his beard black, so too his curly hair, his speech quiet

as of a well-mannered person, and his large eyes like those of Ethiopian holy
men

in the ancient paintings, where pain like a groom and joy like a bride have
intermingled.

His spirit, I sense, is a smile.

Surprise, surprise. A surprise like a midnight sun in the Jezreel Valley.

It is written: Of the more wondrous than you, make no query. I ask nothing.

My dreamed one, my home is your home, don't leave me, I am wanting
without you.

הַמַּרְתֵּף מִתַּחַת לְבֵית הַמִּרְזֵחַ בְּשַׁשְׁטִין,
הָעֹמֶק הָאָפֵל הַזֶּה, אֵיךְ פִּתְאֹם רֵיחוֹ הַקָּרִיר בְּאַפִּי?
תְּלוּיִים בּוֹ מַקְלוֹת סָלָמִי, יַיִן שָׁמוּר בְּחָבִיּוֹת עֵץ,
גַּם בִּירָה, יָארוֹשׁוֹבְּסְקָה, אִם זִכְרוֹנִי זִכָּרוֹן.
כַּמָּה חַיִּים רָאָה הַמַּרְתֵּף הָאָפֵל הַזֶּה?
הַבַּיִת מֵהַמֵּאָה הַשֵּׁשׁ-עֶשְׂרֵה
אוֹ הַשְּׁבַע-עֶשְׂרֵה. הַאִם שֶׁמֶשׁ כְּבוֹר כְּלָא?
הַאִם רָעֲבוּ בּוֹ עַד מָוֶת, בְּעוֹד שֶׁלְּמַעְלָה רָקְדוּ?
מִי דָר בַּבַּיִת הַזֶּה לִפְנֵי שֶׁשָּׂבְּרִי רְכָשׁוֹ בְּיַחַד עִם
אָחִיו הַחוֹרֵג, בַּעַל הַפֻּנְדָּק?
הַאִם רְכָשׁוּהוּ מִיּוֹרְשֵׁי בְּעָלָיו, אִישׁ מִפַּמַלְיַת
מַרְיָה תֶּרֶזָה, כְּסִפּוּרֵי הַמְסַפְּרִים?
הָיָה לָהּ, לַמַּטְרוֹנִית, אַרְמוֹן צַיִד בְּשַׁשְׁטִין,
אוֹתוֹ יִשּׁוּב חֲצִי-כְּפָר-חֲצִי-עֲיָרָה,
יָרִיד גָּדוֹל אַרְבַּע פְּעָמִים בַּשָּׁנָה,
וְגַם קָתֶדְרָלָה עִם אִמָּא קַדִּישָׁא בַּעֲלַת נֵס.
וַהֲרֵי כִּמְעַט נֵס הוּא שֶׁהַיּוֹם, בְּגִיל תִּשְׁעִים
פִּתְאֹם עוֹלֶה בְּאַפִּי רֵיחוֹ שֶׁל אוֹתוֹ מַרְתֵּף
שֶׁאוּלַי פַּעֲמַיִם-שָׁלֹשׁ יָרַדְתִּי בּוֹ בִּימֵי יַלְדוּתִי.
הַאִם מִתְקַצֵּר מִתְאָרֵךְ הַזְּמַן כָּעוֹלֶה עַל רוּחוֹ?
וְלָמָּה לֹא נֵס נוֹסָף וַאֲנִי חַי לִפְנֵי עֲבָרִי,
נֵעוֹר בְּלֵב שָׂמֵחַ?

# THE CELLAR

The cellar under the tavern in Shashtin,

that dark depth, how is its cool scent suddenly what I smell?

Strings of salami hang there, wine stored in wooden vats,

beer too, Yaroshovska, if my memory serves.

How much life did that dark cellar see?

The house was from the sixteenth century

or seventeenth. Was it once used as a prison cell?

Did they starve to death there while others danced above?

Who lived in that house before my grandfather bought it together with

his step-brother, the pub's owner?

Did they buy it from the descendants of the owner, a man of

Maria Theresa's entourage, as the stories go?

She had, the Empress, a hunting palace in Shashtin,

that same half-town-half-village,

a big fair four times a year,

and a cathedral for the Holy Mother of Miracles.

And now it's almost a miracle that today, at the age of ninety

I suddenly smell the scent of that cellar

where in my childhood I went down maybe two or three times.

Does time shorten and lengthen as it wishes?

And why not another miracle that I live before my past,

awakening with a happy heart?

בָּאת עִם הָרְבִיעִיָּה הַפִילְהַרְמוֹנִית
לְנַגֵּן אֶת הַחֲמִישִׁיָּה בְּפָה מִינוֹר שֶׁל בְּרַהְמְס.
לֹא אָהַבְתִּי אָז אֶת בְּרַהְמְס, הָיָה "שָׁמֵן" מִדַּי בִּשְׁבִילִי.
אֲבָל הַפַּעַם הָיָה יָפֶה לְהַפְלִיא.

*

אֵיזוֹ דְּמוּת תְּמִירָה הָיִית!
עוֹד הַיּוֹם אֶפְשָׁר לִרְאוֹת.
הָיִית כְּמוֹ נִצָּן עוֹד טֶרֶם פְּרִיחָתוֹ.
בְּלִבִּי פָּרַחַתְּ. הַמְשַׁכְתְּ לִפְרֹחַ, עַד מְלוֹאֵךְ.

*

הָיִיתִי זָקוּק לְאֵם לְבִתִּי בַּת הַשָּׁלֹשׁ.
אֵיךְ קִבַּלְתְּ עַל עַצְמֵךְ? צְעִירָה בַּת 20.
בָּאת בִּשְׂמָלָה בְּצֶבַע דְּגָנִיּוֹת.
תָּמִיד אָהַבְתִּי צֶבַע דְּגָנִיּוֹת.

*

הָיָה בָּךְ מַשֶּׁהוּ כְּמוֹ בְּאַדְמַת הַמִּרְעֶה בָּאָבִיב,
עֵשֶׂב וּפְרָחִים גְּבוֹהִים מִמֶּנִּי.
הַאִם אָמַרְתִּי: "אֲנִי אוֹהֵב אוֹתָךְ"?
אֵינִי זוֹכֵר. לֹא הָיִיתִי רָגִיל לְהַבִּיעַ רְגָשׁוֹת.

*

## SINCE THEN

You arrived with the philharmonic quartet
to play Brahms' Fifth in F Minor.
I didn't care for Brahms, too "fat" for me.
But this time he was stunning.

\*

What a tall and slender form you were!
One can still see that today.
You were like a bud just before blossoming.
In my heart you blossomed, continued to blossom, into fullness.

\*

I needed a mother for my three-year-old daughter.
How did you take that on? A young woman of 20.
You came in a dress the color of cornflowers.
I always loved the color of cornflowers.

\*

Something in you was like a field in spring,
weeds and flowers taller than me.
Did I say: "I love you"? I don't remember.
I was unaccustomed to speaking my feelings.

\*

אֲבָל כַּמָּה, קָרוֹב לְתִשְׁעִים, עוֹד כּוֹתְבִים
שִׁיר אַהֲבָה?
אַתְּ כַּנָּרָאֶה הָעַרְמוּמִית
שֶׁבַּפְּמוּזוֹת.

*

בַּחֲתֻנָּה שָׁתִיתִי 24 כּוֹסִיּוֹת מִכָּל-בַּכֹּל.
פָּחַדְתְּ שֶׁאֶשְׁתַּכֵּר.
לֹא הִשְׁתַּכַּרְתִּי,
הָיִיתִי נִדְהָם.

*

מֵאָז אֲנִי כְּעֵץ הַשָּׂדֶה.
מֵאָז אֲנִי יוֹדֵעַ לִשְׂמֹחַ.
מֵאָז אֲנִי צָעִיר וְזָקֵן,
זָקֵן וְצָעִיר.

*

עַד הַשֶּׁבֶר הַגֵּאוֹלוֹגִי.
מִי שֶׁשּׁוֹכֵל בֵּן עַד סוֹף יָמָיו שׁוֹכְלוֹ.
הַאִם אֲנִי מַשְׁלֶה אֶת עַצְמִי שֶׁאַתְּ מֵיטִיבָה מִמֶּנִּי
לְגַשֵּׁר עַל פִּי הַתְּהוֹם? גַּם פָּנַיִךְ פִּתְאֹם דְּמָעוֹת.

*

עַכְשָׁו אַתְּ קָמָה בַּבֹּקֶר וְאֵינֶנִּי מַרְגִּישׁ.
אַתְּ מְדַבֶּרֶת אֵלַי וְאֵינֶנִּי שׁוֹמֵעַ.
עֵינַי מִטַּשְׁטְשׁוֹת וְהוֹלְכוֹת. הֵיכָן אַתְּ, בָּבַת עֵינִי?
בּוֹאִי, תְּנִי יָד שֶׁאָקוּם מִן הַמֵּתִים.

But how many nearing ninety still write
love poems?
You are apparently the slyest
of Muses.

\*

At the wedding I drank 24 glasses of everything.
You were afraid I would get drunk.
I didn't get drunk,
I was amazed.

\*

Since then I have been like a tree in the field.
Since then I know how to be happy.
Since then I am young and old,
old and young.

\*

Until the geological rupture.
He who is bereaved of a son is bereft of him to the end
of his days. Do I delude myself that you bridge the abyss
better than I do? Your face too is suddenly tears.

\*

Now you rise in the morning and I don't feel.
You speak to me and I don't hear.
My eyes grow blurrier. Where are you, apple of my eye?
Come, give me your hand so I can rise from the dead.

המושלם לא

הַמֻּשְׁלָם לֹא נָפַל בְּחֶלְקֵנוּ,
אָז לָמָה לְהַעֲמִיד פָּנִים?

בְּעֵינֵי נְמָלָה
אֵזוֹב הַקִּיר גָּבוֹהַּ גָּבוֹהַּ כְּאֶרֶז הַלְּבָנוֹן.

יֵשׁ נָמוּךְ שֶׁהוּא גָּבוֹהַּ
וְגָבוֹהַּ שֶׁהוּא נָמוּךְ.
הַכֹּל תָּלוּי בָּעֵינַיִם הָרוֹאוֹת.

הַרְבֵּה דְּבָרִים אֶפְשָׁר לִרְאוֹת וְלִשְׂמֹחַ
כְּגוֹן עַנְנֵי אָבִיב שֶׁעוֹד לֹא נִבְלְעוּ
בַּכָּחֹל הַחוֹמֵד־כֹּל,
מִשְׁפָּט בְּסֵפֶר שֶׁל חָבֵר קָרוֹב לְלִבְּךָ
לֵאמֹר: "אֵין דָּבָר עָצוּב מִלִּהְיוֹת צוֹדֵק,"
בֶּן שָׁבָא מֵרָחוֹק וּפָנָיו מְאִירוֹת,
מִכְתָּב מִמִּי שֶׁחָשַׁבְתָּ אוֹתוֹ לְמֵת,
וּכְגוֹן הַפָּנִים שֶׁאַתָּה גּוֹחֵן עֲלֵיהֶן
וּמַטְבִּיעַ אֶת שְׂפָתֶיךָ בְּשִׂפְתֵיהֶן,
כְּבָר לֹא אַתָּה.

## THE PERFECT WASN'T

The perfect wasn't ever our lot,
so why pretend?

In the eyes of an ant
the wall's shrub is as tall as the cedars of Lebanon.

There's low that is high
and high that is low.
It all depends on who's looking.

Many things one can see and rejoice
like spring clouds that are not yet swallowed
by the all-coveting blue,
a sentence in a book by a beloved friend
saying: "There is nothing sadder than being right,"
a son who comes from far away and his face shines,
a letter from someone you thought was dead,
and like the face that you lean over
planting your lips on those lips,
no longer you.

הַמַּיִם הַגְּדוֹלִים הַמְזֹהָמִים,
הַיָּם הָאַחֲרוֹן הַמְזֹהָם,
הַיָּם שֶׁלָּנוּ, מִי זִהֵם אֶת הַיָּם שֶׁלָּנוּ
שֶׁהַדָּגִים לֹא יוּכְלוּ עוֹד לִדְגֹּר וְהַצְּמָחִים
הַתַּתְמֵימִיִּים נֶחְנָקִים, מִי? מִי?
מִי זִהֵם אֶת הַשָּׂדוֹת, אֶת הַשְּׁטָחִים הַיְרֻקִּים שֶׁהָיוּ,
מִי אֶת הָאֹשֶׁר, אֶת הַשִּׂמְחָה, אֶת הַצְּחוֹק וְהַחֲבָלִים הַקְּטַנִּים,
אֶת רְעוּת הָרוּחַ? מִי אֶת הַתְּבוּנָה, מִי אֶת שִׁקּוּל הַדַּעַת,
אֶת הָרֶגֶשׁ, אֶת הַיָּדַיִם הַמּוּשָׁטוֹת לַעֲזֹר, מִי אֶת הַיָּדַיִם
בְּדַם יֶלֶד קָטָן? מִי זִהֵם אֶת הַבָּתִּים בִּשְׂחִין הָעַצְמָה, מִי אֶת
הַנְּעָרִים הַנּוֹשְׂאִים מָוֶת עַל גּוּפָם?
מִי? מִי?
מִי אֶת מַרְאֵה הָעֵינַיִם, אֶת כָּל הַיֹּפִי הַזֶּה,
אֶת הַחֶמְלָה?
מִי אֶת הָאָזְנַיִם מִשְׁמַע אֶת הַזְּעָקָה?
זִהוּם הָאֲוִיר שֶׁאָנוּ נוֹשְׁמִים.
זִהוּם הָאֵמוּן שֶׁנָּתַנּוּ.
זִהוּם הַלֵּב הֲכָמֵהַּ.

## THE GREAT WATERS

The great waters, polluted
the last sea, polluted
our sea, who polluted our sea
so the fish can't hatch eggs and the deep-sea
plants are suffocating – who? Who?
Who polluted our fields, the once green spaces,
who polluted happiness, joy, laughter, the small nothings,
the wind's friendship? Who polluted wisdom, reason,
feeling, hands extended to help, who polluted the hands
with a child's blood? Who the houses with the boils of power, who
the young men carrying death on their bodies?
Who? Who?
Who polluted all we see, all this beauty,
and compassion?
Who the ears, deafening them to the screams?
Pollution of the air we breathe.
Pollution of the faith we gave.
Pollution of the heart, yearning.

אֲנִי אוֹמֵר אַל תֹּאמַר

גַּם הַשּׂוֹרְדִים מֵתִים שְׁכוּחִים

אֲנִי אוֹמֵר אַל תֹּאמַר

גַּם יְלָדִים עַכְשָׁו רוֹצְחִים

אֲנִי אוֹמֵר אַל תֹּאמַר

אֲנִי עָנִי, חָשׁוּב כַּמֵּת

אֲנִי אוֹמֵר אַל תֹּאמַר

לֵב הַמָּמוֹן שָׁקֵט שָׁקֵט

אֲנִי אוֹמֵר אַל תֹּאמַר

בּוּשָׁה, בּוּשָׁה, בּוּשָׁה, בּוּשָׁה

אֲנִי אוֹמֵר אַל תֹּאמַר

מִי יֵדַע מַה זֹּאת בּוּשָׁה

אֲנִי אוֹמֵר אַל תֹּאמַר

כִּי בְּגִידָה רוֹדֶפֶת מִרְמָה

אֲנִי אוֹמֵר אַל תֹּאמַר

כִּי לְנוֹפֵל אֵין תְּקוּמָה

אֲנִי אוֹמֵר אַל תֹּאמַר

הָרַע מוֹשֵׁל וְזוֹהֵר

אֲנִי אוֹמֵר אַל תֹּאמַר

נִמְנַעְוֹ תּוֹעֶה כְּעִוֵּר

אֲנִי אוֹמֵר אַל תֹּאמַר

הָאֲדָמָה נוֹשֶׁמֶת דָּם

אֲנִי אוֹמֵר אַל תֹּאמַר

אָדָם שׁוֹב אֵינֶנּוּ אָדָם

אֲנִי אוֹמֵר אַל תֹּאמַר

לְאָן? לְאָן? אֵין כָּאן אֵין שָׁם

אֲנִי אוֹמֵר אַל תֹּאמַר

כֻּלָּנוּ הָפַכְנוּ אָשֵׁם

# LITANY

I say don't say
    The survivors also die forgotten
I say don't say
    They too are killers now, the children
I say don't say
    I am poor, as important as the dead
I say don't say
    The heart of Mammon quietly treads
I say don't say
    *Shame, shame, shame,* and *shame*
I say don't say
    Who knows now what shame is
I say don't say
    That betrayal chases deceit
I say don't say
    There is no rising from defeat
I say don't say
    Evil rules and shines
I say don't say
    He who abstains wanders blind
I say don't say
    The land breathes blood and ruin
I say don't say
    The human is no longer human
I say don't say
    To where? There's no where to be
I say don't say
    We are all now guilty

אֲנִי אוֹמֵר אַל תֹּאמַר

אֲהוּבָה, צְנוּעָה, הֲמוּמָה
הָאָרֶץ תְּלוּיָה עַל בְּלִימָה.

I say don't say
    Beloved, defeated, misled
    This land hangs by a thread.

לא כחל ולא סרק

לֹא כָּחָל וְלֹא סָרָק.
אֶפְשָׁר?
קָשֶׁה לָדַעַת.
וּמַה נִשְׁאָר?
צָרִיךְ לְנַסּוֹת.
גַּם עַל גָּחוֹן?
גַּם עַל גָּחוֹן.
נִשְׁאֶרֶת דְּמוּת? נִשְׁאֶרֶת
אֵיזוֹ דְּמוּת?
אֵיזוֹ תְּנוּעָה.
בָּאוֹר? בַּחֹשֶׁךְ? בָּאוֹר?
קָשֶׁה לָדַעַת.
אֲבָל כָּל עוֹד
מַה?
כָּל עוֹד אֶפְשָׁר
מַה?
כָּל עוֹד אֶפְשָׁר לוֹמַר
מַה?
שֶׁיְּשׁוּב
מִי?
שֶׁיְּשׁוּב וְיִהְיֶה
מִי?
שֶׁיְּשׁוּב וְיִהְיֶה וְנֵדַע
מַה?
לָמָּה הַכֹּל –
כֵּן.

## PLAIN AND UNADORNED

Plain and unadorned.
    Is that possible?
Hard to know.
    And what remains?
One must try.
    Even slithering on one's belly?
Even on one's belly.
    Does an image remain? Does some
    image remain?
What movement.
    In the light? In the dark? In the light?
Hard to know.
    But so long as
What?
    So long as one can
What?
    So long as one can say
What?
    That he'll return
Who?
    That he'll return and be
Who?
    That he'll return and be and we'll know
What?
    Why everything –
Yes.

אַתָּה כּוֹתֵב?

לֹא. אֲנִי לֹא.

אָז מִי כּוֹתֵב?

מִנַּיִן לִי?

אָז מִי אִם לֹא אַתָּה?

לָמָה אֲנִי?

יֵשׁ עוֹד מִישֶׁהוּ בַּחֶדֶר?

אֵינֶנִּי רוֹאֶה.

מָתַי כֵּן?

כֵּן, מָתַי.

בִּזְמַן שֶׁעוֹד הָיְתָה שִׁירָה בָּאֲוִיר?

אוּלַי.

וּמַה יֵּשׁ עַכְשָׁו?

מָוֶת.

אַחַר כָּל הָ

אַתָּה רוֹצֶה מָה?

שִׂמְחָה, לִגְרֹם שִׂמְחָה.

הוֹ, כֵּן, שִׂמְחָה.

שֶׁיִּשְׂמְחוּ קְצָת.

עַל מָה?

עַל מַה שֶּׁאַתָּה כּוֹתֵב.

אֵינְךָ שׁוֹמֵעַ?

מָה?

אֶת הַהִתְאַלְּמוּת.

שׁוֹמְעִים הִתְאַלְּמוּת?

מִי שֶׁמַּקְשִׁיב, שׁוֹמֵעַ.

אֵיזוֹ הִתְאַלְּמוּת?

שֶׁל הַמִּלִּים. הַמִּלִּים הַדּוֹמְמוֹת.

מִי יָכוֹל הָיָה לָדַעַת

כֵּן.

## AFTER BECKETT

Do you write?

    No, not me.

Then who writes?

    How would I know?

Then who if not you?

    Why me?

Is there anyone else in the room?

    I can't see.

When yes?

    Yes, when.

When there was still poetry in the air?

    Maybe.

And what is there now?

    Death.

After all the

    You want what?

Happiness, to cause happiness.

    Oh, yes, happiness.

That they might be a little happy.

    About what?

About what you've written.

    Can't you hear?

What?

    The becoming mute.

You can hear something becoming mute?

    The one who listen, hears.

What is becoming mute?

    The words. The silent words.

Who could have known

    Yes.

מַה מִּלִּים יְכוֹלוֹת לְחוֹלֵל.
כֵּן.
הַקַּיִץ הוֹלֵךְ וְכָלֶה.
בָּרוּךְ הַשֵּׁם.
אַתָּה עוֹד בַּלֹּא שֶׁלְּךָ?
לֹא.
מְאֻחָר. צָרִיךְ לוֹמַר שָׁלוֹם.
מִסְתַּבֵּר.
אֲבָל חֹשֶׁךְ.
יֵשׁ בְּרֵרָה?

What words can make happen.

    Yes.

Summer is fading.

    Thank god.

You are still in your no?

    No.

It's late. We have to say goodbye.

    Seems so.

But the darkness.

    Is there any choice?

# II

# STILL BEFORE

מלאך מתהווה


בְּעוֹלָם הַבֵּינַיִם
מֵהַמַּחְשָׁבוֹת הֲכִי חֲשׁוּכוֹת
עוֹלֶה וְצָף מֵעֵין מַלְאָךְ,
מֵעוֹלָם לֹא רָאִיתִי אֶת פָּנָיו
וְעַכְשָׁו אֲנִי רוֹאֶה
קָו לְקָו, תָּו לְתָו –
אֵיפֹה?
בַּדַּף הַלָּבָן

## ANGEL BECOMING

In the interim world
from within the darkest thoughts
a type of angel rises and floats,
I never saw its face
but now I see it
line by line, note by note –
where?
On the white page

בארץ הצבאים

לָבָן וַאֲפַרְפַּר וְאָפֹר וְתָכֹל
וְיָרֹק שָׁבֵעַ וְחוּם
צִבְעֵי בְּרָאק וְצִבְעֵי
הָעֵמֶק
וְהוּא חֲלוֹם, זֹהַר, וְאוֹרָה
מִתְמַעֶטֶת לְאַט
בַּיּוֹם הַשְּׁלֹשִׁים בְּיָנוּאָר אַלְפַּיִם וְשֵׁשׁ עֶשְׂרֵה
בְּהֶעָרֵב הַיּוֹם. שְׁתֵּי חֲגָלוֹת מְהַדְּסוֹת
לְפָנֵינוּ, לֹא חוֹשְׁשׁוֹת מִמְּכוֹנִיתֵנוּ,
לִימִינֵנוּ בִּקְעָה עֲמֻקָּה עֲמֻקָּה,
בִּקְעַת הַצְּבָאִים,
לֹא צְבָאִים, גַּם לֹא אַיָּלוֹת,
אַף לֹא אַחַת עִם כֶּתֶר קַרְנֶיהָ,
רַק פָּרוֹת זְעִירוֹת קָרוֹב לַפִּסְגָּה
וּמֵעֲלֵיהֶן כּוֹכַב הַיַּרְדֵּן, כַּאוֹכַב אַל־הַוָּוא
וַעֲנָנִים בְּאָפֹר כֵּהֶה וְלָבָן מַעְתִּיקִים
אֶת סְעִיפֵי הַבִּקְעָה וּסְנִיפֶיהָ כְּמוֹ
מִלְחָמָה שֶׁל חֲלוֹם, אַךְ רֶגַע
אֵיזֶה רֶגַע מֵעַל הַיָּרֹק הַמִּתְמַעֵט בְּעַצְמוֹ.
הוֹלֵךְ וּמַחְשִׁיךְ לְאַט,
מַחְשִׁיךְ וְהוֹלֵךְ וְעַיִן קְטַנָּה בּוֹהֶקֶת
כְּמוֹ נִקְרָאָה מִמַּעֲמַקִּים
מִתּוֹךְ הַצֵּל הַמִּתְעַבֶּה, בְּרֵכַת דָּגִים
הִיא אוֹמֶרֶת, וְהִנֵּה וְהִנֵּה קְצָת רָחוֹק יוֹתֵר
עוֹד זַהֲרוּרֵי עֵינַיִם בְּוָרֹד קָלִיל,
מַרְאַת שָׁמַיִם מַוְרִידִים מֵעַל הַגִּלְבֹּעַ
מַוְרִידִים, סְמוּקִים אוֹ מַאֲדִימִים,
מַאֲדִימִים אוֹ מִתְכַּרְכְּמִים

## IN THE LAND OF THE DEER

White and dusky and grey and azure
and a sated green and brown
the colors of Braque and colors of
the Valley
and it's a dream, glory, and light
slowly ebbing
on the 30th of January two thousand and sixteen
at the edges of the day, two partridges hopping around
before us, unafraid of our car,
to our right a deep deep vale
Valley of the Deer,
no deer, also no does,
not even one with her crown of horns
just small cows near the peak
and above them Kochav HaYarden
Star of the Jordan, Kawkab al-Hawa,
and clouds of dark grey and white displacing
the forks and fissures of the valley like
a war of dreams, but calm
what calm above the green deepening on its own.
It's slowly growing darker
getting darker and a small eye glistens
as though calling from out of the depths
from within the widening shadow, a fish pond,
she says, and there just a bit further
more glimmering eyes in light pink,
the sky's mirror pinkening over the Gilboa
becoming pink, flushed or reddening,
reddening or becoming saffron-yellow

מֵאֲחוֹרֵינוּ, וּמִלְפָנֵינוּ הַמַּתָּכוֹת בָּאֲוִיר
מִתְקַבְּצוֹת, נִמְסָגוֹת,
שָׁטוֹת אֶל פֶּתַח הַכִּבְשָׁן
בִּקְצֵה מַעֲרָב
וּכְמוֹ בִּשְׂרֵפַת הַמֵּת
לַהַב מִלְמַעְלָה וְלַהַב מִלְמַטָּה,
נֶתֶךְ נְחֹשֶׁת וּפְלִיז וְגָפְרִית וְאוּלַי
גַּם זָהָב גּוֹלֵשׁ אֶל יַם הָאֵשׁ
עַד הַנּוֹתָר אֵפֶר בִּלְבָד
וְהַחֹשֶׁךְ הַכֹּל יָכוֹל
מִתְפַּשֵּׁט וְהוֹלֵךְ וּמְבַלֵּעַ
לִמְעַט הָאוֹר הַגָּנוּז.

behind us, and before us the metals of the air

gather together, melding

sailing toward the oven's opening

at the western edge

and as with cremation of the dead

a flame from above and a flame from below,

alloy of bronze and brass and sulfur and perhaps

gold too flowing toward the sea of fire

till grey alone remains

and the omnipotent darkness

slowly spreads and swallows all

but for the hidden light.

לִכְתֹּב הַיּוֹם שִׁיר
כְּמוֹ לֶאֱחֹז בְּקַשׁ
שֶׁלֹּא לִטְבֹּעַ .

*

Writing a poem today is
like clutching a straw
to not drown.

שניים בחשאי

מַדְהִים. מַדְהִים
מָה?
הַיֹּפִי הַזֶּה
שֶׁל מָה?
שֶׁל Vespro della Beate Vergine
תְּפִלַּת עַרְבִית שֶׁל מוֹנְטֶוֶרְדִי.
יֹפִי מַדִּיר מַחְשָׁבוֹת.
תָּמִיד?
שׁוּב וָשׁוּב.
אֶצְלְךָ.
מִי שֶׁלֹּא נִפְתָּח, לֹא קוֹלֵט.
אֵיךְ?
אֲנִי, כְּשֶׁשָּׁמַעְתִּי לָרִאשׁוֹנָה
כָּל חַלּוֹנוֹת לִבִּי הָאֲפֵלִים הוּאֲרוּ לְפֶתַע.
אַל תַּפְלִיג כְּדֵי כָּךְ!
אֵינֶנִּי מַגְזִים
וְעַכְשָׁו בְּאָזְנַיִם צְרוּדוֹת?
גַּם. אֲבָל
אֲבָל מָה?
כְּלוּם.
כְּלוּם מָה?
שֶׁיּוֹם אֶחָד לֹא אֶשְׁמַע עוֹד.
אַתָּה לֹא תִּשְׁמַע?
לֹא אֶשְׁמַע.
וְאַתָּה תִּהְיֶה עוֹד אַתָּה?

64

Amazing. Amazing.
    *What?*
All this beauty.
    *What beauty?*
Of Vespro della Beate Vergine
Monteverdi's Vespers.
Beauty that casts away all thoughts.
    *Always?*
Again and again.
    *For you.*
Whoever doesn't open up, can't comprehend.
    *How?*
Me, when first I heard it,
all the dark windows of my heart lit up at once.
    *Don't get carried away!*
I don't exaggerate.
    *And now with hoarse ears?*
Also. But
    *But what?*
Nothing.
    *Nothing what?*
That one day I'll hear it no more.
    *You won't hear it?*
I won't hear it.
    *And will you still be you?*

רכבת העמק, אגדת סתיו

מִי יוֹדֵעַ כַּמָּה זְמַן עוֹד נִרְאֶה
אֶת הָעֵמֶק הַיָּפֶה הַזֶּה
אוֹקֵר וְכָתֹם וְיָרֹק וְחוּם, תְּכֵלֶת
עִם עֲנָנִים לְבָנִים גַּם קְצָת שְׁחֹרִים
מִי יוֹדֵעַ כַּמָּה זְמַן
נֹאכַל מִן הַחִטָּה הַגְּדֵלָה בּוֹ
וְנָשִׁיר הָעֵמֶק הוּא חֲלוֹם וְגַם
פֵּרוֹתָיו כְּגוֹן שְׁקֵדִים מִמַּטָּעֵי הַשְּׁקֵדִים
שֶׁפּוֹרְחִים לֹא עַכְשָׁו, אֲבָל אוּלַי
בָּאָבִיב הַבָּא
עָלֵינוּ לְטוֹבָה אוּלַי.
וּמֵהַקִּשׁוּאִים וְהָאֲבַטִּיחִים שֶׁבִּשְׂדוֹתֵינוּ
מִבֵּית אַלְפָא וְעַד נַהֲלָל
נוֹסַעַת רַכֶּבֶת הָעֵמֶק אַחֲרֵי מְנוּחַת
שִׁבְעִים שָׁנָה כַּלָּה חֲדָשָׁה לְמֵהַדְּרִין.
סַפְּרוּ: לִפְנֵי שִׁבְעִים שָׁנָה בָּחוּר רָאָה בָּהּ
בַּחוּרָה יָפָה, הִתְאָהֵב בָּהּ וְהִיא יָלְדָה תִּינוֹק
כְּשֶׁהָרַכֶּבֶת הִגִּיעָה לַתַּחֲנָתָהּ הַסּוֹפִית.
סִפּוּרִים כָּאֵלֶּה מְסַפְּרִים בַּקּוֹמָה הַשְּׁנִיָּה
בָּהּ יָשַׁבְנוּ וְרָאִינוּ בְּכֶרֶם זֵיתִים
אֶת צַמָּרוֹת עֲצֵי הַזַּיִת מִלְמַעְלָה
גַּלִּים גַּלִּים בָּרוּחַ וְגַם בִּדְבָרִים אֲחֵרִים
נִכְנְסָה הָרוּחַ לֹא תָּמִיד רָעָה
מִי יוֹדֵעַ כַּמָּה זְמַן עוֹד
וְרַכֶּבֶת הָעֵמֶק שׁוּב תָּנוּחַ שִׁבְעִים שָׁנָה כִּי
לֹא תִהְיֶה כְּדָאִית מִבְּחִינָה כַּלְכָּלִית אֶלָּא אִם
יִבָּנוּ בָּעֵמֶק נְמַל תְּעוּפָה וְלֹא יִהְיֶה עוֹד עֵמֶק.

66

# THE VALLEY TRAIN, AN AUTUMN FAIRY TALE

Who knows how long we'll still see
this beautiful valley
ochre and orange, green and brown, light-blue
with white clouds a few black ones too
who knows how long
we'll eat of the wheat growing here
and we'll sing *the valley is a dream* and
its fruit too, like almonds from the almond groves
that bloom not now, but maybe
next spring
that will come in good time maybe.
And of the zucchini and watermelon in our fields
from Beit Alfa to Nahalal
the valley train is traveling after
a seventy-year rest all brand new.
As the tale was told: on this train seventy years ago
a boy saw a beautiful girl, fell in love with her and she
gave birth to a baby when the train reached its final station.
Tales like this are being told on the upper tier
where we sat looking out at the olive groves
at the tree-tops from above
waves and waves in the wind that blows also through
other things not always melancholic
who knows how long before
the valley train will rest again seventy years because
it'll be economically unviable unless
they build an airport in the valley and then there'll be no more valley.

הָיֹה הָיָה שֶׁזּוּג בָּא בַּיָּמִים, טוּבְיָה, מִתְקָרֵב לְ־93
וְגְלִילָה, בַּת 84, נָסְעוּ יַחַד בְּרַכֶּבֶת הָעֵמֶק וְאִם לֹא מֵתוּ בָּאֲמְבּוּהָא
בִּכְפַר יְהוֹשֻׁעַ הֵם חַיִּים עוֹד הַיּוֹם בְּיַחַד בָּאֲשֶׁר
וּמִי יִתֵּן וְכָךְ יַמְשִׁיכוּ שָׁנִים רַבּוֹת עַל אַדְמַת הָעֵמֶק
וְלֹא יִפָּרְדוּ גַּם לֹא בְּתוֹכָה אִם תְּנֻתָּר.

6.10.16

Once upon a time there was an old couple, Tuvia, nearing 93, and
Galila, 84, who traveled together on the valley train and if they haven't died
    in the throng
at Beit Yehoshua then they're still living together happily ever after
and may they continue thus for many years to come on this valley's earth
never to be separated also not when within it, if it is spared.


6.10.16

# אֵין מַצָּב

בְּעִיר שֶׁל קֹדֶשׁ וּשְׁאוֹל, בְּאֶרֶץ הַמֶּלֶךְ
בַּסְּתָו הַמַּפְרִיחַ שִׂנְאָה כְּאַפְנָה אַחֲרוֹנָה
שִׂנְאָה בָּהּ צָפִים כָּל הַפְּחָדִים, כָּל הַתִּסְכּוּלִים
כְּמוֹ בְּבִיוּב סָתוּם, אֵין מַצָּב שֶׁלֹּא יִירוּ
בְּמִי שֶׁרוֹצֶה לִרְצֹחַ אוֹ בְּמִי שֶׁחוֹשְׁבִים כִּי רוֹצֶה.
רֶצַח הוּא רֶצַח הוּא רֶצַח הוּא רֶצַח
אָמְרָה מִי שֶׁאָמְרָה בְּפָרִיז שֶׁל רֵאשִׁית הַמֵּאָה הַקּוֹדֶמֶת
אוֹ יְכוֹלָה הָיְתָה לוֹמַר.
אֵיזֶה עָתִיד יָכוֹל הָיָה לַעֲמֹד לְנֶגֶד עֵינֵיהֶם
שֶׁל הַדּוֹקְרִים הַצְּעִירִים לְהַחֲרִיד
וְאֵיזֶה עָתִיד לְנֶגֶד עֵינֵיהֶם שֶׁל מְבַצְּעֵי הַלִּינְץ'
שֶׁבְּשֶׁל צֶבַע עוֹרוֹ תָּקְעוּ בּוֹ כַּדּוּרִים שִׁשָּׁה וְאַחַר כָּךְ
בְּעָטוּ, בָּטְשׁוּ, זִינּוּ אֶת הַגּוּף הַמְּפַרְפֵּר כְּמוֹ דָּג.
אֵל נְקָמוֹת, שֵׁד נְקָמוֹת. טַעַם נְקָמָה כְּטַעַם זוּג
שֶׁלֹּא מִן הַשָּׁמַיִם, דָּבוּק לְאֵין הַפָּרֵד.
עַד מָה מַרְחִיבָה אֶת הַדַּעַת שׁוּעָפַט בְּלִי שׁוּעָפַט
וְכַמָּה יָפָה לְלֹא סִיג הָאָרֶץ בְּלִי הֶרֶג הֶרֶג הֶרֶג
שָׁם וָכָאן. הֶרֶג סַכִּין וְהֶרֶג אֵשׁ, הֶרֶג אֶבֶן וְהֶרֶג רוֹבֶה.
לֹא תָּמִיד יֵשׁ אִזּוּן בֵּין נִגּוּדִים.
כַּמָּה טוֹב לֵב יָכוֹל הָיָה לִהְיוֹת הָאָדָם
אִלּוּלֵא רַע הַלֵּב.
וְאֵיזֶה גַּן עֵדֶן יָכוֹל הָיָה לִהְיוֹת
אִלּוּ אֵי פַּעַם הָיָה.

# NO WAY

In a city of holiness and hell, in the land of Moloch,
in an autumn spreading hatred like the latest fashion,
hatred in which all the fears, all the frustrations, float to the surface
like backed-up sewage, there's no way they won't shoot
the one who wants to murder, or the one they think wants to.
Murder is murder is murder is murder
said she who said this in Paris at the beginning of the previous century
or could have said it.
What future could have been before the eyes
of the stabbers, so appallingly young
and what future before the eyes of those who lynched
him whose skin color led them to pump six bullets into him then
kick, bash, and maul his body flopping around like a fish.
Vengeful God, Vengeful Devil. The taste of revenge is like the taste of a
     coupling
not made in heaven, stuck together and inseparable.
How satisfying is Shu'afat without Shu'afat
and how boundlessly beautiful is this land without the killing killing killing
here and there both. Knife killings and ax killings, stone killings and gun
     killings.
There isn't always parity between the sides.
How much good-heartedness there could have been in man
were it not for all the evil.
And what a paradise this could have been
if only it had ever been.

חלום בלהות

הֵם הִתְחִילוּ. הֵם הִתְחִילוּ. וְלָכֵן
חָרַשְׁנוּ וְזָרַעְנוּ אֶת אַדְמוֹתֵיהֶם
עַד שֶׁצָּצוּ מִתּוֹכָן כְּפִרְחֵי הַשָּׂדֶה
תִּינוֹקוֹת תִּינוֹקוֹת אֵם וְאָב אֵין.
כְּרוּחַ הַיָּם מְחַפְּשׂוֹת נָשִׁים אֶת בְּנֵיהֶן בֵּין
הֲרִיסוֹת הֲרִיסוֹת הֲרִיסוֹת עַד הָאֹפֶק הָאָפֵל
הַבָּזוּי, הָרוֹעֵד, הַמְּנֻדֶּה
מִשָּׁמַיִם מְמֹרָקִים לְמִשְׁעִי אֵין צֵל
אֵי לִכְבֹּשׁ אֶת הַפָּנִים בַּקַּרְקַע וְאֵי לְהִסְתַּתֵּר
מִפְּנֵי עַצְמֵנוּ כִּי אֵין לְהַפְסִיק וּלְוַתֵּר
חֲמוֹר נֶחְנַק רֹאשׁוֹ בַּחוֹל
אַרְבָּעוֹתָיו בּוֹעֲטוֹת בָּאֲוִיר עַד שֶׁאֵינוֹ יָכוֹל
יְדֵי יְשִׁישִׁים עֲקֻמּוֹת מְפַשְּׁטוֹת קַלּוֹת
כְּצֵל אֶל עוֹפוֹת הַטֶּרֶף וְהָאֵשׁ
יוֹם אַחַר יוֹם וּבְכָל הַלֵּילוֹת
בַּלְשָׁלֶשֶׁת הַזֹּאת אֵין אֵין וְאֵין יֵשׁ.
חֲלָלִים חֲלָלִים עֵץ לְיַד עֵץ
יַלְדָּה מְדַלֶּגֶת עַל קַו הַקֵּץ.

## GAZA NIGHTMARE

They started it. They started it. And so
we sowed and seeded their lands
till there sprouted there like wildflowers
babies upon babies mother and father none.
Women like sea-winds search for their sons among
the ruins ruins ruins as far as the horizon dark
and demeaned, trembling, banished
from the sky smoothly emptying no shadow
no place to cover faces in shame, there's no hiding
from ourselves because one mustn't stop and yield
a donkey smothers its head in the sand
its four legs kicking in the air until it cannot
the gnarled hands of the old are slightly outstretched
like a shadow toward the birds of prey and the fire
day after day and every night
in these chicken droppings there's not not and not is.
All the slain, dead upon dead, tree beside tree
a girl skipping at the edge of the end.

ויקרא

1. ויקרא

צַעַר הַצָּרַעַת
מִתְפַּשֵּׁט
עַל כָּל חֶלְקָה טוֹבָה
צוֹבֵעַ לָבָן
כְּחוֹל שֶׁל מַעְלָה
שֶׁאֵינוֹ עוֹד מַעְלָה
לָבָן עָבֵשׁ
כְּמוֹ אוֹתוֹ לָבָן
בַּמַּעֲבָר הַמַּרְתִּפִי אֶל
הָאֵינָדַעַת.

הַלְוַאי
זֵכֶר, קֹרֶט שֶׁל זֵכֶר
קְדֻשָּׁה

# VAYIKRAH

1. *VaYikrah* (And He Called)

The plague's anguish
spreads
over every good portion
paints white
the blue above
which is no longer above
a moldy whiteness
like that same whiteness
in the cellared corridor toward
the notthought.

If only
a remnant, a remnant speck
of holiness

2. קרבן

לֹא
לֹא עוֹד
לֹא עוֹד קָרְבָּן
לֹא הָעֵינַיִם הַשְּׁתוּקוֹת
קְרִיעַת קוֹל אַחֲרוֹן
וְהֶעָשָׁן הַזֶּה, הָאֵפֶר
לֹא
כָּל הַנָּרוּק
לֹא
לֹא עוֹד הָאֵפֶר הַזֶּה
בּוֹ אָנוּ שׁוֹקְעִים וְטוֹבְעִים
טוֹבְעִים וְשׁוֹקְעִים.

2. *Korban* (Sacrifice)

No
not another
not another sacrifice
not the silenced eyes
last rending of voice
and this smoke, the ash
not
all that is cast off
no
no more of this ash
in which we are sinking and drowning
drowning and sinking.

3. זהב

הָה, הַזָּהָב
בְּאֶרֶץ שְׁמָמָה
מָה עוֹשֶׂה הַזָּהָב
בְּאֶרֶץ שְׁמָמָה?
מִנַּיִן בָּא?
מֵהָרָעָב, מֵהַצָּמָא?
מֵעֵגֶל הָאֵלָה?
– כָּל הַגְּבָעוֹת רָקְדוּ
וְהָהָר נִזְדַּעֲזַע –

הֲיֹפִי הֶזֶּה הַזָּהָב
בְּאֶרֶץ שְׁמָמָה
הַיֹּפִי בְּלִבּוֹ חֵטְא
הַזָּהָב, הָה, הַזָּהֵב

כְּרוּבִים חוֹשְׁקִים בִּכְנָפַיִם זְקוּרוֹת
לֹא זָזִים
לֹא נוֹסְקִים, כָּנָף בְּכָנָף
רוֹכְבִים עַל תֵּבָה
מַה יֵּשׁ בַּתֵּבָה?
רֵיחַ נִיחוֹחַ? רוּחַ קָדְשָׁה?
יָהוּ צוֹהֵל רוּחַ הַמִּדְבָּר
מִסוֹף הָעוֹלָם וְעַד סוֹפוֹ
יָהוּ

3. Gold

Oh, the gold
in a land laid waste
what is the gold doing
in a land laid waste?
Whence did it come?
From the hunger, the thirst?
From the deified calf?
– All the hills danced
and the mountains were set atrembling –

This golden beauty
in a land laid waste
the beauty in its heart is sin
of the gold, oh, goldening

The yearning cherubim with wings thrust out
don't move
don't ascend, wing to wing
they ride on the ark
what is in the ark?
Sweet aroma? A spirit of holiness?
Ho, the desert wind exclaims and exults
from the end of the world to its end
Ho

תמיהות

אַתָּה רוֹצֶה אֶת יוֹסְל? יוֹסְל אֵינֶנּוּ.
לֹא בַּבַּיִת? מָתַי יַחֲזֹר?
הוּא הָלַךְ בְּלִי לְהַגִּיד.
הָלַךְ לְאָן?
מִי יָכוֹל לָדַעַת. אוּלַי אֶל חֲלוֹמוֹתָיו.
וְלָמָּה אֶתְמוֹל לַחֲלוֹמִי?
כָּל כְּלֵי הַמִּטְבָּח נֶעֶלְמוּ
הַקַּנְקַנִּים עָפוּ לָעֲנָנִים, הַפַּמְפִּיּוֹת צָחֲקוּ מֵרָחוֹק
אוֹ בָּכוּ. לֹא קַל לְהַבְחִין.
וְכָל הַכּוֹבָעִים הַמְשֻׁלָּשִׁים.
וְהָעֵינַיִם, הָעֵינַיִם הַיָּפוֹת הַשְּׁחֹרוֹת
שֶׁרוֹאוֹת אֶת הַכֹּל וְלֹא רוֹאוֹת כְּלוּם.
וְגַם הַיָּם. אֵיפֹה הַיָּם?
וְהַמַּסֵּכוֹת.
הַמַּסֵּכוֹת הִסְתַּתְּרוּ מֵאֲחוֹרֵי מַסֵּכוֹת.

אֵיךְ כָּךְ, אֵיךְ?
עִם מִי אֲדַבֵּר

## WONDERINGS

Are you looking for Yosl? Yosl isn't here.
Not at home? When will he be back?
   He left without saying.
Left to go where?
   Who knows. Maybe to his dreams.
And why yesterday into my dreams?
All the kitchen utensils disappeared
the kettles flew up to the clouds, the peelers laughed from afar
or cried. It's hard to tell.
And all the three-cornered hats.
And the eyes, the beautiful black eyes
that see everything and see nothing.
And also the sea. Where is the sea?
And the masks.
The masks hid behind masks.

How has this happened, how?
With whom will I talk

אָמֵן

הַבּוֹגֵד הַנִּבְגָּד
הַמְּשַׁקֵּר הַמְּשֻׁקָּר:
הָלְאָה! הָלְאָה!
אֵיזֶה הָלְאָה?
לְאָן הָלְאָה
בָּאֲוִיר הַצָּהֹב?
אֶל הָאָחוּ שֶׁהָיָה?
אֶל הַטְּלָאִים שֶׁנּוֹלְדוּ?
אֶל הַצִּפֳּרִים שֶׁנָּשְׁרוּ?

בְּעָמְדֵנוּ, הֲגַם מְעַט כְּפוּפִים – דַּיֵּנוּ.
בְּעֵינֵינוּ הָרוֹאוֹת הַטְּרוּטוֹת – דַּיֵּנוּ.
בְּאָזְנֵינוּ הַכִּמְעַט שׁוֹמְעוֹת – דַּיֵּנוּ.
בְּשָׁכְבֵנוּ וּבְקוּמֵנוּ – דַּיֵּנוּ.
בְּזָכְרֵנוּ אֶת שֵׁם אַהֲבָתֵנוּ – דַּיֵּנוּ.
בְּשֵׁן וָעַיִן – דַּיֵּנוּ.
בְּכָרְעֵנוּ עַל בִּרְכֵּינוּ – דַּיֵּנוּ.
בְּלִבֵּנוּ הַמַּרְחִיב וּמֵצֵר – דַּיֵּנוּ.
בְּלִבֵּנוּ הַחוֹשֵׁשׁ, הֶחָרֵד, הַיָּרֵא – דַּיֵּנוּ.
אָמֵן.

## AMEN

The betrayer who is betrayed.
The deceiver deceived.
Away! Away!
What away?
Away to where
in the yellow air?
To the meadow that was?
To the lambs just birthed?
To the fallen birds?

In our standing up, though a little bent – *dayenu*.
With our eyes seeing even blurred – *dayenu*.
With our ears almost hearing – *dayenu*.
Upon our lying down and our rising up – *dayenu*.
On our remembering our beloved's name – *dayenu*.
Even as battered and broken – *dayenu*.
On our bending down upon our knees – *dayenu*.
In our heart that expands and contracts – *dayenu*.
In our worried heart, fearful and afraid – *dayenu*.
Amen.

נער

הַשָּׁמַיִם נִפְתָּחִים.
מַלְאָכִים בּוֹכִים.
פְּנֵי הַנַּעַר הִלְבִּינוּ וְהָלְכוּ.
הוֹרְגוֹ הָרוּג.
הַכּוֹכָבִים נוֹשְׁרִים כְּעָלִים מֵעֵץ הַפֶּקָן.
פָּנָיו הִלְבִּינוּ וְהָלְכוּ. הוֹרְגוֹ לֹא הָרוּג.
אֱלֹהִים מְגַלְגֵּל אֶת הַזְּמַן.
יִהְיֶה וְהָיָה.
פְּנֵי הַנַּעַר מַלְבִּינוֹת.
אַחַר כָּךְ קָם וְרוֹכֵב עַל אוֹפַנָּיו.
כָּךְ הָיָה וְכָךְ יִהְיֶה.
אֵיךְ יוֹדְעִים.
אֱלֹהִים מְגַלְגֵּל אֶת הַזְּמַן.
אֱלֹהִים – אֵיזֶה חֲלוֹם!
אֱגוֹזֵי הַפֶּקָן מִתְפַּקְעִים.
הָרוֹפְאִים עֲמֵלִים עַל הַנֵּס.

## A BOY

The skies open.

Angels weep.

The boy's face grew white and faded.

He who killed him has been killed.

The stars fall like leaves from the pecan tree.

His face grew white and faded. He who killed him

hasn't been killed. God keeps time turning.

He will be and he was.

The boy's face grows white.

Afterwards he rises and rides away on his bike.

That's what was and what will be.

How do we know.

God keeps time turning.

God – what a dream!

The pecans are bursting forth.

The doctors work for the miracle.

בֵּין כֶּסֶה לֶעָשׂוֹר

*

רֹאשׁ הַשָּׁנָה בָּא
עִם זוֹ שֶׁחָלְפָה. אֵין גְּבוּל
בֵּין יֵשׁ לְאַיִן.

*

רוּחוֹת צְלָלִים
שָׁטִים בְּאוֹר שְׂרֵפָה.
תּוּגָה מוּזָרָה.

*

דְּבָרִים תְּמוּהִים בֵּין
כֶּסֶה לֶעָשׂוֹר. יֵשׁ מִי
אֲשֶׁר יְדָעָם?

*

צִיץ נוֹבֵל: פֶּרַח –
רוּחַ מְרַחֶפֶת לָהּ
מַעְלָה, מַטָּה.

*

פְּנֵי יָנוּס לַזְּמַן
שֶׁבֵּין כֶּסֶה לֶעָשׂוֹר
פָּנִים וְאָחוֹר

# DURING THE DAYS OF AWE

\*

New Year arrives
with that which passed. No line
between what is and is not.

\*

Shadowing-winds
wander in the light that has waned.
Strange grief, strange sorrow.

\*

Perplexing things between
the New Moon and Tenth Day. Does
someone know them?

\*

A wilting blossom: a flower –
wind-fluttering there
upward, then down.

\*

Time is Janus-faced
during the Days of Awe, it looks
forward and back

# אקוודור

בְּ-Cuenca שֶׁבְּאֶקְוָדוֹר קָתֶדְרָלָה בְּשֵׁם "אֶל סַגְרָרִיוֹ" מֵ-1554
וְקָתֶדְרָלָה "נוּאֵבוֹ" מְפֹאֶרֶת בַּעֲלַת אַרְבַּע כִּפּוֹת גְּדוֹלוֹת וְזֹאת
בִּגְלַל טָעוּת הַנְדָּסִית שֶׁמָּנְעָה לְהַרְכִּיב כִּפָּה דְּגִמַת פִירֶנְצֶה.

בָּעִיר הַתַּחְתִּית בְּסֵפֶר הָאוֹרְחִים שֶׁל בֵּית מָלוֹן זוֹל רָשׁוּם שֵׁם בְּנִי.

קָרוֹב לְמֶרְכַּז הָעִיר זוֹרֵם הַנָּהָר Tomebamba. עִיר יָפָה Cuenca.
בַּפֶּרֶק הַלְאֻמִּי קָיָס שְׁנֵי אֲגַמִּים נִשְׁקָפִים זֶה בָּזֶה.

יֵשׁ לְשַׁעַר שֶׁגַּם בֵּית חוֹלִים יֵשׁ בְּ-Cuenca
וּבוֹ אוּלַי מִטְבָּחִים סְמוּיִים מִן הָעַיִן,
שָׁם מַפְרִידִים כָּבֵד מִמָּרָה, רֵאוֹת, וּשְׁחָלוֹת, מַפְרִידִים
לֵב מִכְּלָיוֹת וְכָל פֶּרֶט אָרוּז בְּקֻפְסַת מַתֶּכֶת מֻקְפֵּאת
מוּכָנָה לְמִשְׁלוֹחַ. לִגְוִיּוֹת צְעִירוֹת עֲדִיפוּת רִאשׁוֹנָה.

תַּעְתּוּעֵי מֹחַ מְטֹרָפִים יֵשׁ בְּ-Cuenca, אֶקְוָדוֹר. אֶקְוָדוֹר הוֹרוֹר,
חֲלוֹמוֹת בְּעוּתִים וְאֵיפֹה אֵין?

אַךְ גַּם אִיֵּי גָלַפָּגוֹס שַׁיָּכִים לְאֶקְוָדוֹר עִם צַבֵּי הָעֲנָק בְּנֵי מֵאוֹת בַּשָּׁנִים
וְעוֹד מִינֵי מִינִים שֶׁל בַּעֲלֵי חַיִּים וּצְמָחִים יְחוּדִיִּים.
שׁוֹדֵד הַיָּם אַמְבְּרוֹז קָאוּלִי גִּלָּה אוֹתָם בְּ-1684.
לְדַרְוִוין שִׁמְּשׁוּ כְהוֹכָחָה לְתוֹרַת הָאֵבוֹלוּצְיָה.
תִּמְצָא שָׁם אֲנָדִמִים לָרֹב וְלֹא תִמְצָא שָׁם דּוּ-חַי, גַּם לֹא אֶחָד.

הַבִּנְיָמִין שֶׁלִּי בִּקֵּשׁ לְבַקֵּר בְּאִיֵּי גָלַפָּגוֹס.
הוּא הָיָה צָעִיר סַקְרָן,
רָצָה לִרְאוֹת חַיִּים בִּבְתוּלֵיהֶם.

ECUADOR

In Cuenca in Ecuador there's a Cathedral called El Sagrario from 1554
and an ornate "Nuevo" Cathedral with four large domes and that's
due to an engineering error which prevented erecting a Florence-styled dome.

In the lower city in the guest book of a cheap hotel you'll find my son's name.

Near the city center the Tomebamba River flows. It's a pretty city, Cuenca.
In El Cajas National Park two lakes mirror each other.

One can assume that there's also a hospital in Cuenca
and in it there are maybe morgues hidden from sight.
There they separate liver from pancreas, lungs and ovaries, they separate
heart from kidneys and every item is packed up in a steel cold box
ready for transfer. Young corpses get first attention.

Wild hallucinations in Cuenca, Ecuador. Ecuador Horror,
night terrors, aren't they everywhere?

But also the Galápagos Islands are in Ecuador with their giant turtles
hundreds of years old and other distinctive types of flora and fauna.
The pirate Ambrose Cowley discovered them in 1684.
For Darwin they served as proof of evolution.
You'll find there numerous endemic species, and not a single amphibian, not
    even one.

My Benjamin wanted to visit the Galápagos Islands.
He was young and curious,
he wanted to see the world in its first innocence.

עִם הַבּוֹר הַשַּׁחֹר
עִם הָרִיק הַגָּדוֹשׁ
עִם הַתְּהוֹם הַזֹּאת בְּתוֹכִי
מִכֹּבֶד הָאַהֲבָה
מֵעָרְגָּה שֶׁאֵינָהּ נִכְנַעַת
לַבֵּן הָאוֹבֵד
עַכְשָׁו עַל סַף
חֲלִיפָתִי.

\*

With the black pit
With the emptiness overflowing
With this abyss inside me
From the weight of love
From longing that is unrelenting
For the lost son
Now at the threshold
Of my passing.

יש צעקות

יֵשׁ צְעָקוֹת מַרְעִידוֹת אֶת הָאֲוִיר.
יֵשׁ צְעָקוֹת כְּמוֹ דְּמָמָה.
הָאָב אָבַד.
פִּסּוֹת הַדֶּשֶׁא חֲוָרוֹת.
אֶבֶן כְּסֶלַע.
יֵשׁ אֱלֹהִים בַּשָּׁמַיִם?
אֱלֹהִים נָתַן, אֱלֹהִים לָקַח?
מִלִּים כְּמוֹ סְמַרְטוּטֵי נְיָר שָׂרוּף בָּרוּחַ.
גֵּיהִנֹּם.

עֶרֶב קָסוּם יוֹרֵד עַל הַנּוֹף וּמַכְנִיסֵנִי תַּחַת כְּנָפָיו,
תְּחִלָּה כְּתֻמּוֹת, אַחַר כָּךְ בּוֹרְדוֹ כְּמוֹ מֶרלוֹ.
אֶפְשָׁר לְהָבִין?
אֶפְשָׁר.
וְאַחַר כָּךְ?

## THERE ARE SHOUTS

There are shouts that make the air tremble.
There are shouts that are silence.
The father is lost.
The grass patches are pale.
Rocks like boulders.
Is there a God above?
God gave and God took away?
Words like burnt paper-rags in the wind.
*Ja'hannam. Infernus.*

An enchanted evening descends on the hills and takes me
under its wings, first they're orange, then crimson like a Merlot.
Is it conceivable?
It is.
And afterwards?

אֵם וָאָב

אֵין לִרְאוֹת אֶת הָאֵם וְלֹא אֶת הָאָב.
גַּם אֶת בִּתָּם אֵין לִרְאוֹת.
לֹא בְּיַעַר הַגְּזַרְקָה שֶׁסָּבִי נָהַג לְהַשְׁכִּים וּלְבַקֵּר בּוֹ
אֵצֶל "עֵצָיו" הָאֲדַמְדַּמִּים
– מֶה עָלָה עַל דַּעְתּוֹ יוֹם אֶחָד לְהַמְרִיא וְלִהְיוֹת
צִפּוֹר זְעִירָה כְּעָנָן זָעִיר? –
לֹא בִּנְקַּת טְרַנְבָה, לֹא בְּמַחוֹז סֶנִיצָה.
לֹא בִּירוּשָׁלַיִם, עִיר הַקֹּדֶשׁ שֶׁל הַגֵּיהִנּוֹם
לֹא בְּעֵמֶק יִזְרְעָאל.
לֹא בְּשַׁשְׁטִין בָּרְחוֹב הַמּוֹבִיל אֶל בָּזִילִיקַת
הַבְּתוּלָה שֶׁל שִׁבְעַת הַמַּכְאוֹבִים.
לֹא בְּיוּנִי 1942.
וְלֹא בְּאוֹקְטוֹבֶּר 2015.
הַמָּקוֹם חָלוּל עַד כְּדֵי לִרְאוֹת דַּרְכּוֹ.
כַּמָּה רֵיק הַכֹּל!
אֵיזֶה לֹא כְלוּם.

94

## MOTHER AND FATHER

They can't be seen, neither the mother nor the father.

Also their daughter can't be seen.

Not in Gazárka Forest which my grandfather used to rise early to visit

"his" red-hued trees

– What on earth was he thinking to take flight one day and become

a bird as tiny as a tiny cloud? –

Not in the Trnava region, not in Senica district.

Not in Jerusalem, the Holy City of Hell

not in the Jezreel Valley.

Not in Shashtin on the street leading to the Basilica

of The Virgin of the Seven Sorrows.

Not in June 1942.

And not in October 2015.

The place is so hollow one can see through it.

How empty it all is!

What nothing.

בלי שם

עֵינָיו בְּעֵינַי
גּוּפוֹ גּוּף שֶׁל חֲלוֹם
קוֹלוֹ לְפָנִים
הוּא יוֹשֵׁב בֵּין אֶגְרוֹפֵי לִבִּי
לֹא אַנִּיחֶנּוּ
עַד מוֹתִי.

## UNTITLED

His eyes are in my eyes
His body is the body of a dream
His voice within
He sits between the fists of my heart
I will not let him go
Till I die.

תצלום

הוּא לְנֶגֶד עֵינַי. הָאוֹר
מֵאֲחוֹרָיו. קוֹלוֹ לֹא
נִשְׁמָע. גַּם לֹא
הֶגֶה אֶחָד.

אֶצְבְּעוֹתָיו עַל קְלִידֵי פְּסַנְתֵּר
אֲנִי זוֹכֵר: שׁוּבֶּרְט, אִמְפְּרוֹמֶנְטוֹ בְּפָה מִינוֹר
אֵיזוֹ דְּמָמַת מֵיתָרִים

אֲנִי מַבִּיט. מַבִּיט. מִתְעַרְעֵר. פָּנַי
נוֹפְלוֹת. אֵין בִּי עוֹד כֹּחַ לְהָרִים.

## PHOTOGRAPH

He's before my eyes. The light's
behind him. His voice isn't
heard. Not even
a single sound.

His fingers are on the piano keys
I remember: Schubert, Impromptu in F Minor
What silence of strings

I look and look. I wake. My face
falls. I have no more strength to lift it.

# הָאֵם

הַאִם אֶצְטָרֵף אֲלֵיכֶם בְּקָרוֹב
אוֹ רַק בְּ"עוֹד קְצָת עוֹד" כְּמוֹ שֶׁאוֹמֵר גּוּרִי
אוֹ אֲפִלּוּ בְּ"עַד קְצֵה עוֹד"?
הַיָּמִים אֵינָם טוֹבִים.
צְעִירִים רַבִּים כָּל כָּךְ נֶהֱרָגִים,
בְּלִי סוֹף נֶהֱרָגִים.
אָז לָמָּה לְהַאֲרִיךְ עוֹד וְעוֹד יָמִים שֶׁל הַיָּשִׁישׁ הַזֶּה?

הַפְּרֵדָה מֵאֲהוּבַי וּמִנּוֹפַי –

רַק רֶמֶז מַחְשָׁבָה עָלֶיהָ כְּפֶצַע בְּלִבִּי
וְיוֹם בְּלִי מַכְאוֹבֵי הַגּוּף – יוֹם הוֹדָיָה.
רֹאשִׁי צָלוּל. וְיוֹם אַתָּה בְּיַחַד, הַגְּלוּיָה לִי בְּסוֹדָהּ,
יוֹם כָּלוּל.
וְגַם הַמּוּזִיקָה עַל אַף אָזְנַי הָעֲרֵלוֹת עוֹד מְחַיָּה נַפְשִׁי
וְהַתְּמוּנוֹת בַּחֲדָרֵינוּ, לָאַחֲרוֹנָה "שִׁיבַת הַבֵּן הָאוֹבֵד"

– הֲרֵי נֶחֱרְתָה בִּי בְּצַעֲקָתִי עִם בּוֹאִי לָעוֹלָם.
וְאֵין הַמְּלָטוּת.

אִם אֶצְטָרֵף אֲלֵיכֶם, אֲבוּדַי,
לֹא תִּהְיוּ עוֹד אֲבוּדַי.
אַף לֹא אֶחָד.

## WILL

Will I join you soon
or just in "a little more more" as Gouri says
or even "till the edge of more"?
These days are not good ones.
So many young are being killed,
no end to the dead.
So why extend the days of this old man more and more?

The departure from my beloveds and from my landscapes –

Just the hint of this thought is a wound to my heart
and a day with no physical pain –is a day of praise.
My mind is clear. And a day together with you, revealed to me in your secret,
is a perfect day.
Also the music, despite my dulled ears, still revives my soul
and the pictures in my room, lately the "Return of the Prodigal Son"

– after all it was etched in me with my cry the day I entered the world.
And there's no escape.

If I join you, my lost ones,
you will no longer be my lost ones.
Not a single one.

בְּשָׁעָה

בְּשָׁעָה שֶׁהוּא חוֹלֵם עָלַי
בְּשָׁעָה שֶׁאֵינוֹ מֵזִיז עֵינָיו מִמֶּנִּי
בְּשָׁעָה שֶׁנִּגְרָר אַחֲרַי כְּצֵל
בְּשָׁעָה שֶׁהוּא מְנַסֶּה לָגַעַת בִּי
בְּשָׁעָה שֶׁשׁוֹלֵחַ בִּי אֶת יָדוֹ
בְּשָׁעָה שֶׁיַּעֲלֶה וְיָבוֹא
לְהַכּוֹתֵנִי עַד חָרְמָה –
אוֹ אָז, אָנָּא, בְּאַחַת,
לֹא בִּשְׁתַּיִם, בְּאַחַת!

כֵּן יְהִי רָצוֹן,
אָמֵן.

102

## AT THE HOUR

At the hour he dreams about me
At the hour he doesn't take his eyes off me
At the hour he drags behind me like a shadow
At the hour he tries to touch me
At the hour he reaches out to me
At the hour he rises up
to annihilate me –
Oh then, please, in one fell swoop,
not two, but one!

May it be done,
Amen.

# III

# MORE NO MORE

זיקוקין דינור, שיר בנוסח ישן


בְּרֶדֶת רֶכֶב הַשֶּׁמֶשׁ אֶל שִׁכְחַת לַיְלָה
וְאוֹרוֹ הַמֵּת שֶׁל הַסַּהַר עוֹלֶה לְאַטּוֹ
בּוֹא רֵעַ שְׁעוֹת הִרְהוּרַי וְנֵיטִיב אֶת לִבֵּנוּ
בְּיַיִן זָהֹב כְּזִיווֹ שֶׁל יָרֵחַ מָלֵא
וְהִנֵּה אֵין סְפֹר כּוֹכְבֵי צִבְעוֹנִין נוֹרִים לַחֲשֵׁכָה
חֲגִיגַת חַיֵּינוּ: זִקּוּקִין דִּי־נוּר.

# FIREWORKS, A SONG IN OLD STYLE

As the Sun's chariot descends into Night's oblivion
And the dead light of the Crescent slowly ascends
Come, friend of my meditative hours, and we'll succor our hearts
With wine as golden as the full Moon's lustrous glow
And now countless multicolored stars are shot in the dark
Celebration of our lives: Sparks of light.

ביום הארוך של השנה

בַּיּוֹם הָאָרֹךְ בַּשָּׁנָה אֲנִי רוֹצֶה לוֹמַר
חֲזֹר וָשׁוֹב הַחַיִּים יָפִים. יָפֶה לִחְיוֹת.
וְהַמִּלִּים מְקַפְּצוֹת בִּגְרוֹנִי וְאֵינָן חֲפֵצוֹת לָצֵאת.
מַדּוּעַ, מַדּוּעַ אֵינָן?
הַאֵין זֶה הַטּוֹב בָּעוֹלָמוֹת
אֲפִלּוּ תָּלוּי עַל בְּלִימָה
הַשֶּׁמֶשׁ עֲדַיִן לְמַעְלָה
וְהָעֵשֶׂב לְמַטָּה
וְתַחַת לָעֵשֶׂב יֵשׁ אֲדָמָה וְאֶבֶן מֵעַל הָאֵשׁ
אֵיזוֹ שִׂמְחָה שֶׁכָּךְ וְלֹא הָפוּךְ
וְתוּכַל אֻשְׁכָּרָה לֶאֱהֹב
גַּם אִם אַתָּה אִלֵּם כְּמוֹ עַכְבָּר מִתְחַבֵּא
אֲבָל הִנֵּה הַמִּלִּים יוֹצְאוֹת מִן הֶחָסוֹם
וּבְגִיל 94 אַתָּה כּוֹתֵב, חֲבָל עַל הַזְּמַן
שִׁיר חָדָשׁ, שִׁיר שֶׁל יַרְגָּזִי
שִׁיר הַלֵּל.

## ON THE LONGEST DAY OF THE YEAR

On the longest day of the year I want to say
again and again, life is beautiful. It's beautiful to be alive.
And the words hop around in my throat but don't wish to come out.
Why, why don't they?
Is this not the best of all worlds
even suspended as it is over nothing
the sun is still above
the grass below
and under the grass there's earth and stone above the fire
what joy that it's thus and not the other way around
and you can love, for real,
even if you're as mute as a mouse in hiding
and now the words are emerging from the blockage
and at the age of ninety-four you're writing, it's wild,
a new poem, song of a tufted titmouse
a song of praise.

מחתרת

הָבָה נִחְיֶה בַּמַּחְתֶּרֶת, סְמוּיִים מֵעֵין הָרוֹדֵף
וּנְהַלֵּל אֶת הָאֲדָמָה, אֶת שָׁדוֹתֶיהָ כָּל עוֹד נִתָּן לִרְאוֹתָם,
אֶת תִּפְאֶרֶת אַלּוֹנֶיהָ וְאַלּוֹתֶיהָ, גַּם אֶת אֲרָנֶיהָ אִם לֹא נִשְׂרְפוּ
נְהַלֵּל אֶת תִּפְרַחַת עֲצֵי הַשָּׁקֵד בָּאָבִיב וְאֶת צֹהַב עֲלֵי הַפִּקָּנִים בַּסְּתָו,
אֶת הַבּוּגֶנְוִילֵאוֹת בְּצִבְעֵיהֶן מִכָּתֹם עַד סָגֹל,
וְאֶת נַחַל דָּן הַשּׁוֹצֵף

וְשׁוֹעֵט כְּעֵדֶר בִּיזוֹנִים לְבָנִים אֲפִלּוּ בַּקַּיִץ,
נְהַלֵּל אֶת כּוּר הַמַּצְרֵף שֶׁל קַיְצָהּ,
אֶת הַכִּנֶּרֶת, כָּל עוֹד הַיָּמָּה קַיֶּמֶת כְּעֵין הַתְּהוֹם וּרְאִי הַמָּרוֹם
בְּרָכָה הֵם יִשְׁרֵי הַדַּעַת, וּנְקִיֵּי הַכַּפַּיִם שֶׁקּוֹלָם לֹא נִשְׁמַע
וְאַשְׁרֵינוּ עַל שֶׁבְּתוֹכֵנוּ טוֹבֵי לֵב הַמּוֹשִׁיטִים יָדָם לְחַסְרֵי אוֹנִים,
הָבָה נְגַלֶּה אֶת הַסְּמוּיִים וְעִמָּם מִי שֶׁהַשֶּׁקֶר אֵינוֹ לֶחֶם חֻקָּם
וּנְהַלֵּל אֶת פֶּרַח הַמִּדְבָּר, יָחִיד אֵין שֵׁנִי לוֹ בַּפְּלָנֶטָה שֶׁלָּנוּ,
אֶת יָם הַמֶּלַח, בְּטֶרֶם יִיבַּשׁ עַד תֹּם.
מַה יָּפָה הָעֲרָבָה בְּלִי נַחַל אַשָׁלִים
הַמַּזְרִים חָמְצָה קַטְלָנִית וְחוֹנֵק כָּל חַי בִּגְלַל בֶּצַע כֶּסֶף.
נְהַלֵּל אֶת מִדְבָּרֶיהָ שֶׁהֵם פָּנָיו הַחֲרוּשׁוֹת שֶׁל מִי שֶׁמֵּעֵבֶר לַשָּׁמַיִם
וְאֶת שְׁמֵי לֵילוֹתֶיהָ עַל רִבְבוֹת נִקְבֵי הָאֹפֶל,
הָבָה נִחְיֶה בַּמַּחְתֶּרֶת.

UNDERGROUND

Come, let's live in the Underground, hidden from the oppressor's eye
and we'll praise the earth, her fields, so long as they remain visible,
and the splendor of her oaks and her terebinths, also her pines if they're not
  burned down
we'll praise the bloom of the almond trees in spring and the yellow pecan
  leaves in the fall,
and the bougainvillea in their hues from orange to violet,
and the Dan River stomping
and stamping like a herd of white bison even in the summer,
we'll praise the burning crucible of her summers,
and the Sea of Galilee, so long as the sea exists like eye of the abyss and
  mirror of the sky.
A blessing are the honest and the uncorrupted whose voices are not heard
and blessed are we that among us are the kindhearted who extend help to the
  helpless,
let's reveal the hidden and those for whom deceit is not their daily bread
and we'll praise that desert flower, singular on our planet,
the Sea of Salt, before it's drained to nothing.
How lovely is the Arava desert without Ashalim Creek
flowing with toxic acid and suffocating all life for profit and greed.
We'll praise her deserts which are the furrowed face of whoever is beyond
  the sky
and we'll praise her night skies with its myriad piercings of darkness,
Come, let's live in the Underground.

איכה

יִשְׂרָאֵל
הָאָרֶץ הַמֻּבְטַחַת
כֻּלֵּךְ תִּקְוָה וְסִכּוּי כְּמַטַּע עֲצֵי תֹמֶר
אֵיכָה הָפַכְתְּ
אֶרֶץ בָּהּ הָאֱמֶת מַפְנָה עֹרֶף לְעַצְמָהּ
עַד כִּי שֶׁהָיָה לֹא הָיָה?
עוֹד נוֹפַיִךְ נִפְלָאִים לָעַיִן.
עוֹד פּוֹרְחִים יְסוּרַיִךְ כִּכְלִיל הַחֹרֶשׁ.
אֶרֶץ הַפְּרֵדוֹת
עוֹד לִבֵּךְ פּוֹעֵם.
עַד אָנָה
עַד מָתַי

*EIKHA* / O HOW

Israel

The Promised Land

All hope and prospects like an orchard of Palms

O how have you become

A land where truth turns its back on itself

Till what was, wasn't?

Still your landscapes are glorious to the eye.

Still your sufferings blossom like the Judas tree.

Land of leave-takings

Still your heart beats.

How long

Till when

כל הסבל

כָּל הַסֵּבֶל הַזֶּה
כָּל הַצַּעַר
כָּל הַסֵּבֶל וְהַצַּעַר הַזֶּה לַשָּׁוְא
הָאִמָּהוֹת מְכֻוָּצוֹת חֲשָׁשׁ
הָעֵינַיִם הַסְּתוּרוֹת
כָּל הַטֵּרוּף הַזֶּה
לַשָּׁוְא לַשָּׁוְא
הָאָבוֹת מַסְתִּירֵי לִבָּם
מַעֲמִידֵי פָּנִים
כָּל הָאָרֶץ הַזֹּאת מְשֻׁגַּעַת דָּם
לַשָּׁוְא לַשָּׁוְא
הַפָּנִים הַצְּעִירִים אֶפְרֵי עִתּוֹן
אוֹי פְּנֵי הַנְּעָרִים הַצִּבְעוֹנִיִּים
אוֹי
אוֹי עַל שֶׁצִּבְעָם דָּהָה
הַצְּחוֹק הַמְצֻלָּם, הַנְּעָרוֹת
וְהַנָּשִׁים הַצְּעִירוֹת
הַחֲבוּקִים הַנְּשִׁיקוֹת
לַשָּׁוְא לַשָּׁוְא
אוֹי הַשִּׂנְאָה הַזֹּאת הָאוֹכֶלֶת אוֹתָנוּ חַיִּים
אוֹי הַחַיִּים הַפּוֹרְחִים הַכְּמוּשִׁים הָאֵלֶּה
כָּל הָאֲבַדּוֹן הַזֶּה
כָּל הָאֲבַדּוֹן הָעִוֵּר הַזֶּה
שֶׁאֵין מִמֶּנּוּ מוֹצָא.
וְאוֹיָה, אוֹיָה שֶׁאֲנִי כּוֹתֵב כָּל זֹאת

## ALL THE SUFFERING

All this suffering
all the sorrow
all this suffering and sorrow in vain
the fear-clenched mothers
the disheveled eyes
all this madness
in vain in vain
the fathers hiding their hearts
pretending
this whole blood-crazed land
in vain in vain
the young faces a newspaper-grey
oh the colorful faces of youth
oh
how their colors fade
their photographed laughter, the girls
and the young women
the kisses the hugs
in vain in vain
oh this hatred eating us alive
oh these withered blossoming lives
all this ruin
all this blind ruin
from which there is no way out.
And oh, alas that I am writing all this

טיוטה לחזון אחרית הימים
בלי שמץ שירה


קְצָת מַרְגּוֹעַ.
בְּגָבְהֵי הַהִימָלָיָה?

עַל מָה נֶהֱרָגִים? עַל מָה?
עַל הַיֹּפִי שֶׁיֵּשׁ בַּחַיִּים.
עַל מָה?
קָשֶׁה לִשְׁמֹעַ בָּרוּחַ הַזֹּאת.
עַל מָה?

הַשּׁוֹלְטִים אוֹמְרִים: עַל שֶׁלֹּא לִשְׁכֹּחַ אֶת הַפַּחַד.
הַנִּלְחָבִים אוֹמְרִים: עַל גְּאֻלַּת עַצְמָם וְאֶרֶץ הָאָבוֹת.

אָה, גְּאֻלָּה...

אֶרֶץ הָאָבוֹת מְקַדֶּמֶת דְּנָא אוֹהֶבֶת דָּם.
מְשִׁיחֵי שֶׁקֶר צָצִים כְּפִטְרִיּוֹת אַחֲרֵי הַגֶּשֶׁם.

לְהִתְעַלֵּם.
לֹא עוֹזֵר.
לִשְׁכֹּחַ.

אֶפְשָׁר לִשְׁכֹּחַ
נַעַר כְּמוֹ אוֹר שֶׁל חֶסֶד בֵּין הַשְּׁמָשׁוֹת?

הָאָבוֹת נֶאֱמָנִים לְחַבְרֵיהֶם הַמֵּתִים.
הָאִמָּהוֹת מְהַסְּסוֹת.


116

## DRAFT FOR AN END-OF-DAYS VISION
## WITHOUT A TRACE OF POETRY

*A little rest and recovery.*
In the Himalayan heights?

*Being killed for what? For what?*
For the beauty there is in life.
*For what?*
*It's hard to hear in this wind.*
*For what?*

The Rulers say: To never forget the fear.
The Zealots say: For their own redemption and the Forefathers Land.

*Ah, redemption …*

The Forefathers Land, from antique days loving blood
*False prophets sprouting up like mushrooms after the rain.*

Ignore.
*Doesn't help.*
Forget it.

*Can one forget*
*youth like the light of grace at dusk?*

The fathers are loyal to their dead friends.
The mothers are hesitant.

הָאָבוֹת יַקְרִיבוּ אֶת בְּנֵיהֶם.
הָאִמָּהוֹת תְּבַכֶּינָה אֶת בְּנֵיהֶן.
הַבָּנִים יַקְרִיבוּ אֶת בְּנֵיהֶם.
לְשֵׁם הַשַּׁקְרָנִים
וְנוֹשְׂכֵי הַנֶּשֶׁךְ.
כִּי כָּךְ.

* על פי סרט דוקומנטרי: קבוצת נפגעי טראומה מ"צוק איתן" מנסים ריפוי בהקפת ההימליה על אופניים.

The fathers will sacrifice their sons.

The mothers will wail for their sons.

The sons will sacrifice their sons.

For the sake of the liars

and the usurers.

Because.

---

* From the documentary film *Palsar Himalaya*, about a group of Israeli veterans suffering from PTSD, trying to heal while on a motorcycle journey through the Himalayan Mountains.

קמטים

כַּמָּה יָפִים הַקְּמָטִים בְּפָנֶיךָ!
בְּאֵיזֶה סֵדֶר מוּפְתִּי נִשְׁכְּבוּ זֶה בְּצַד זֶה.
מְלֵאֵי חַיִּים עַל טוּבָם וְסִבְלָם,
כַּמָּה זִכְרוֹנוֹת שֶׁמֵּעוֹלָם לֹא פָּתְחוּ פֶּה,
שַׁחַר נְעוּרִים כְּפַס אוֹר דַּק בָּאֹפֶק,
אֲהָבוֹת שֶׁהָיוּ, שֶׁיֶּשְׁנָן, אַכְזָבוֹת, יָגוֹן,
כַּמָּה שִׂמְחָה כְּבוּשָׁה, כַּמָּה חֶמְדָּה,
שְׁאִיפוֹת שֶׁנִּתְמַמְּשׁוּ וְכָאֵלֶּה שֶׁלֹּא.
פָּנֶיךָ מַסְלוּל כּוֹכָבִים מְקֻטָּע
וְעֵינֵי מְלַטְּפוֹת.

## WRINKLES

How beautiful are the wrinkles on your face!
With what exemplary order they lay down beside each other.
Filled with life in all its goodness and suffering,
how many memories that have never spoken,
the dawn of youth like a slender strip of light on the horizon,
loves that were, that are, disappointments, anguish,
how much joy stored, how much severity,
aspirations that were fulfilled and those that weren't.
Your face is the fragmented orbit of stars
and my eyes caress.

עוֹפוֹת נַפְשִׁי, עוֹף־הוּא, עוֹף־הִיא
עָפִים בְּחַלּוֹנִי
עָתִים כִּצְלָלִים
עָתִים פְּגוּעֵי פִּגְיוֹן הַשֶּׁמֶשׁ הַשּׁוֹקַעַת
וְנוֹצוֹתֵיהֶם הַלְּבָנוֹת אֲדֻמּוֹת
יֵשׁ וְצוּרָתָם הָיְתָה שְׁקִיפוּת, יֵשׁ
שֶׁשְּׁקִיפוּתָם נִרְאֲתָה
עֵינַי מְצֻעָפוֹת
כַּמָּה רָצִיתִי לוֹמַר
לְעוֹף־הִיא עִם פְּנֵי אִמִּי
בּוֹאִי בּוֹאִי
אֲבָל גְּרוֹנִי נִחַר
עָפוּ אֶל עַל מְמַשְׁקוֹף חַלּוֹנִי
נֶעֶלְמוּ
הַאִם בָּאוּ לוֹמַר לִי מַשֶּׁהוּ?
הַאִם לְהָכִין אוֹתִי לַשָּׁנָה?
הֱיוּ שָׁלוֹם, עוֹפוֹת נַפְשִׁי
עוֹף־הוּא, עוֹף־הִיא
שָׁלוֹם שָׁלוֹם
שַׁבָּת שָׁלוֹם

# FRIDAY

Birds of my soul, he-bird, she-bird
fly past my window
sometimes like shadows
sometimes disarmed by the daggers of the setting sun
and their white feathers are red
there are those whose form was transparence, and those
with transparence visible
my eyes are veiled
how I longed to say
to she-bird with my mother's face
come here, come here
but my throat was parched
they flew skyward from my window frame
disappeared
did they come to tell me something?
to get me ready me for bed?
Farewell, birds of my soul
he-bird, she-bird
farewell and shalom
*shabbat shalom*

שליחים

כְּמוֹ פֵּרוֹת שֶׁנָּשְׁרוּ וְהִשְׁחִירוּ
נָפְלוּ מֵהָעֵצִים בְּבֵית הַקְּבָרוֹת הַיְהוּדִי שֶׁל פְּרָאג
עוֹרְבִים עוֹרְבִים וְנָסְקוּ כְּאִלּוּ הָיוּ עוֹפוֹת הַחוֹל.

הָיִינוּ שָׁם עִם יוֹסְל שֶׁבָּא לְהָכִין אֶת תַּעֲרוּכַת קַפְקָא שֶׁלּוֹ
וְנִפְגַּשְׁנוּ עִם בְּנוֹת אוֹטְלָה שֶׁשָּׂרְדוּ: עִם וֵרָה שֶׁגַּם חֲזוּתָהּ
גַּם דֶּרֶךְ סִפּוּרָהּ הִזְכִּירוּ אֶת דּוֹדָהּ, וְעִם הֶלֶן
שֶׁנִּשְּׂאָה לְצַ'כִי כְּמוֹ אִמָּהּ וְהָיְתָה רוֹפְאַת פּוֹעֲלִים.

הַאִם כָּל זֶה הִתְרַחֵשׁ?
מַמָּשׁ וְלֹא מַמָּשׁ מִשְׁתַּלְּבִים בִּי מִדֵּי פַּעַם.
אֲבָל הֲרֵינִי רוֹאֶה אֶת עַצְמִי בְּמוֹ עֵינִי
מִסְתּוֹבֵב בֵּין הַקְּבָרִים הָעַתִּיקִים וְיוֹסְל אוֹמֵר:
שֵׁשׁ קוֹמוֹת זֶה עַל זֶה קְבוּרִים כָּאן.
אַחַת שֶׁלֹּא מִבְּנוֹת יִשְׂרָאֵל שָׂמָה פֶּתֶק עַל קֶבֶר הַמַּהֲרַ"ל.

אַךְ מַה פִּתְאֹם נָחֲתוּ הַיּוֹם שְׁלֹשָׁה
שְׁחֹרִים כְּהֶבֶל הַשָּׂטָן וְנֶעֶמְדוּ עַל הַדֶּשֶׁא הַגָּדוֹל
לִפְנֵי בֵּיתֵנוּ כְּמוֹ בָּאוּ לְהוֹדִיעַ דְּבַר מָה?

אֲנִי מַשְׁקִיעַ אֶת רֹאשִׁי הַיָּשִׁישׁ בְּסִפְרָהּ שֶׁל שִׁיבָטָה טוֹיוֹ הַיְשִׁישָׁה:
"אֶשָּׁאֵר כָּאן עוֹד קְצָת, יֵשׁ לִי כַּמָּה דְּבָרִים לַעֲשׂוֹת"

וְלִבִּי שָׂח אֶל הַשְּׁלֹשָׁה וְאוֹמֵר לִי מַה שֶּׁהֵם שָׁתְקוּ.

124

## MESSENGERS

Like fruit that fell and blackened
they dropped from the trees in the Jewish Cemetery in Prague
crows upon crows and then they rose as though phoenixes.

We were there with Yosl who had come to prepare his Kafka exhibit
and we met with the daughters of Ottla who survived: with Vera whose
face and story-telling ways both evoked her uncle, and with Helene
who like her mother had married a Czech and was a workers' physician.

Did it all happen?
Substance and not substance intertwine in me from time to time.
But here I am seeing myself with my own eyes
walking between the old graves and Yosl is saying:
They are buried here one atop the other six stories deep.
Someone, not a daughter of Israel, puts a note on the grave of the Maharal.

But why have these three suddenly landed here today
as black as the devil's breath and here they stand on the grassy common
before our house as though they've come to announce something?

I sink my old head into the book by old Toyo Shibata, she who wrote:
"I'll stay here just a bit longer, there are still some things left to do"

and my heart bows toward the three and tells me what they kept silent.

עודני

יָדַעְתִּי כִּי הַבִּלְתִּי נִתָּן לְהֵאָמֵר
בִּלְתִּי נִתָּן לְהֵאָמֵר.
חַגְתִּי סְבִיבוֹ
כִּסְבִיב חֹר שָׁחֹר
לוֹמַר בִּזְמַן חָשׁוּךְ
יֵשׁ רִגְעֵי אוֹר, הַלֵּל לַחַיִּים.

שׁוּרוֹת הַשִּׁיר
אִיִּים קְטַנִּים שֶׁל זְמַן
מֻקָּפֵי אֵלֶם

כְּמוֹ אֲחוֹרֵי הַחֲלָקִים הַלְּבָנִים
שֶׁל צִיּוּרֵי פִיֶּרוֹ דֶּלָה פְרַנְצֶ׳סְקָה.
אֵין אֵין בְּלִי יֵשׁ. אֵין יֵשׁ בְּלִי אֵין

עוֹדֶנִּי כָּאן. (מִין חֲלוֹם?)
מָוֶת, מַהוּ?

## I AM STILL

I knew that the unsayable is
unsayable.
I orbited it
like around a black hole
in order to say in dark days
there are moments of light, praise for life.

The lines of the poem
are tiny islands of time
surrounded by muteness

like behind the white spaces
in Piero della Franscesca's paintings.
There is no isn't without there is. There is no is without there isn't.

I'm still here. (A kind of dream?)
Death, what is it?

הוּא הוֹלֵךְ בְּשָׂדוֹת

הוּא הוֹלֵךְ בַּשָּׂדוֹת.
בְּהִתְקָרְבוֹ רוֹאִים
פָּנָיו תוֹלָעִים.
צַוָּארוֹ כְּשֶׁל נֶשֶׁר פְּגָרִים.
גּוּפוֹ קוֹרֵן בְּנֹגַהּ כְּחַלְחַל־יְרַקְרַק.
הַשִּׁבֳּלִים בְּשׁוּלֵי דַּרְכּוֹ מַאֲדִימוֹת.
בְּעָבְרוֹ מַשִּׁירִים הָעֵצִים בֶּן רֶגַע אֶת יַרְקוּתָם.
בְּעָרִים שֶׁהוּא חוֹצֶה קוֹרְסִים הַבָּתִּים לְתוֹךְ עַצְמָם.
הוּא הוֹלֵךְ קוֹמְמִיּוּת.
גַּפָּיו כְּשֶׁל חַיָּל רוּסִי בְּמִצְעַד נִצָּחוֹן.
מַעְלָה מַטָּה מַעְלָה מַטָּה.
הוּא מַרְכִּיב מִשְׁקְפֵי שֶׁמֶשׁ כֵּהִים גַּם בַּחֹשֶׁךְ.
הוּא צוֹעֵד לְלֹא הֶפְסֵק יוֹמָם וָלַיְלָה
אֵינוֹ פוֹנֶה שְׂמֹאלָה, אֵינוֹ פוֹנֶה יָמִינָה.
לִפְעָמִים נִפְרָם גּוּפוֹ וְרוֹאִים אֶת הַשֶּׁלֶד.
אַחַר כָּךְ שׁוּב נֶחְתָּם.
לִנְשִׁימוֹתָיו רֵיחַ שֶׁל רָקָב.
עַל הַיָּם הוּא מַבִּיט כְּחוֹלֵם.
כְּשֶׁאוֹמְרִים לוֹ שָׁלוֹם אֵינוֹ עוֹנֶה.
הוּא הוֹלֵךְ וְהוֹלֵךְ.

## HE WALKS IN THE FIELDS

He walks in the fields.

When he comes near, you can see

his face is worms.

His neck is like remains of a carcass.

His body shines with a bluish-greenish light.

The stalks along the way where he walks turn red.

As he passes by, the trees in an instant shed their green.

In the cities that he crosses houses implode.

He walks proud and erect.

His limbs like those of a Russian soldier in a victory parade.

Up down up down.

He wears opaque sunglasses also when it's dark.

He marches without stopping day and night

doesn't turn left, doesn't turn right.

Sometimes his body comes undone and you can see his bones.

Afterwards he's sealed up again.

His breath smells like rot.

He gazes at the sea like a dreamer.

When you greet him he doesn't answer.

He walks and walks.

אֶל

אַל תְּחַפֵּשׂ אֶת קִרְבָתִי
אֲנִי בָּא לִקְרַאת
עוֹד מְעַט
תָּקִין
אֵיכְשֶׁהוּ
מַיְשִׁיר מַבָּט
חוֹשֵׁשׁ וְלֹא
חוֹשֵׁשׁ
מִי יָכוֹל לָדַעַת
אָנָּא
בְּרֶגַע
כִּי מַה טַעַם שֶׁלֹּא
– אִם אֵין אֶל מִי –
לְהִשְׁתַּחֵל אֶל תּוֹךְ גָּלַבִּיָּה
כְּגֶרְקְכּוּס הַצַּיָּד
אֶל תּוֹךְ כֻּתֹּנֶת הַמֵּתִים שֶׁלּוֹ
אוֹ מוּטָב: כְּמוֹ בִּגְלִישַׁת גַּלִּים, בְּ־surfing
לִגְלֹש אֶל הַלֹּא־כְלוּם.
אָמֵן.

## DON'T

Don't seek me out
I am coming toward
in a little while
functioning
somehow
forward-looking
afraid and not
afraid
who can know
please
peacefully
because what's the point of not – if there's not toward whom –
to slip into a *galabiya*
like the Hunter Gracchus
slipped into his death shrouds
or better yet: as in surfing the waves
to surf into the nothing.
Amen.

עיניים

בְּנִי, בִּנְיָמִין שֶׁלִּי,
גַּם אִם אֶעֱצֹם אֶת עֵינַי
הַכְּאֵב עַל הֵעָלְמוּתְךָ
אֵינֶנּוּ עוֹצֵם אֶת עֵינָיו.
חֶסְרוֹנְךָ מְכַרְסֵם
יוֹם יוֹם
אַט
אַט
אֶת כִּלְיוֹתַי וְלִבִּי.

הַנּוֹף הַלֵּילִי כְּמַטְלִיּוֹת קְרוּעוֹת.

שׁוּב וָשׁוּב עֲבָרִי חוֹזֵר אֵלַי
כְּמוֹ זוּג הַיַּרְגָּזִים אֶל קִנּוֹ בְּסֻכַּת בֵּיתֵנוּ.
שׁוּב וָשׁוּב מוֹשִׁיט זְרוֹעוֹת אֲרֻכּוֹת
אֶל אֲחוֹתִי עַל עֵינֵי הָאַיָּלָה שֶׁלָּהּ
שֶׁלָּבְנָן תָּכֹל כְּמוֹ רֵאשִׁית הַשַּׁחַר הַקֵּיצִי,
אֶל אָבִי הַמַּנִּיחַ אֶת עֵינָיו עָלַי כְּמוֹ שׁוֹאֲלוֹת "לָמָה?"
אֶל אִמִּי הָאוֹמֶרֶת בְּעֵינַיִם שֶׁל מַיִם מְעֻנִּים
"אִם אֵינְךָ רוֹצֶה לִנְסֹעַ, אֵינְךָ צָרִיךְ."

לֹא רָצִיתִי. נָסַעְתִּי.

EYES

My son, my Benjamin,
even if I close my eyes
the pain at your disappearance
will not close its eyes.
Your absence gnaws away
at my mind and heart
bit by
bit
day after day.

The night landscape is like ripped rags.

My past returns to me again and again
like the two tufted titmice to their nest in our eaves.
Again and again I extend long arms
toward my sister with her doe eyes
their whites a blue like the budding of dawn on a summer's day,
toward my father resting his eyes on me as though asking "why?"
toward my mother who is saying with eyes of tortured waters
"If you don't want to leave, you don't have to."

I didn't want to. I left.

חָזַרְתִּי
הָלַכְתִּי לַיַּעַר
בָּאתִי לַיַּעַר
נִכְנַסְתִּי לַיַּעַר
הַיַּעַר הָיָה מָלֵא חֹשֶׁךְ
כְּשֶׁנָּמוֹג הַחֹשֶׁךְ
עָמַד שָׁם בַּיִת
אוּלַי אַרְמוֹן
עָשׂוּי אֲוִיר
הָאֲוִיר עָשׂוּי מַרְאוֹת
כָּל חַיַּי הִשְׁתַּקְּפוּ בָּן בֶּן רֶגַע
מִי מְחַכֶּה שָׁם?
מִי מְחַכֶּה לִי שָׁם?
מִי? מִי?

# ON READING GRIMMS' FAIRY TALES IN THEIR ORIGINAL

I returned

I went to the forest

I arrived at the forest

I entered the forest

The forest was full of dark

When the darkness ebbed

there stood a house

maybe a castle

made of air

the air was made of mirrors

my entire life was reflected in them at once

Who is waiting there?

Who is waiting for me there?

Who? who?

נבו

הַמִּישׁוֹר

הָיָה לְעָקֹב

עֶזְרִי מֵאַיִן יָבוֹא

נָשָׂאתִי עֵינַי

הִשְׁפַּלְתִּי

יָגַעְתִּי

תָּעִיתִי

מָעַדְתִּי

נִכְשַׁלְתִּי

נוֹאַשְׁתִּי

הִתְעַקַּשְׁתִּי

עָלִיתִי

הִגַּעְתִּי

עַד

NEVO

The level plain
Became rugged
My help from whence will it come
I lifted up mine eyes
I cast low
I toiled
I strayed
I stumbled
I failed
I despaired
I persevered
I rose up
I reached
Until

זִכָּרוֹן הַבִּלְתִּי־נִתָּן־לְהֵאָמֵר
מְכַרְסֵם בַּמִּלִּים הַמְנַסּוֹת לָגַעַת
שׁוּב וָשׁוּב.

הַקָּרְבָּן אֵינוֹ שׁוֹכֵחַ אֶת מִי שֶׁבִּקֵּשׁ
לִטֹּל אֶת נַפְשׁוֹ?
אֵיזֶה מִין כִּשּׁוּף זֶה?

הַחַזָּאִים הִבְטִיחוּ גֶּשֶׁם מָחָר
אֶפְשָׁר יִהְיֶה לִנְשֹׁם אֲוִיר נָקִי.

*

Memory of the unspeakable
eats away at the words that try to touch
again and again.

The victim doesn't forget the one who
sought to kill him?
What kind of sorcery is this?

The forecasters have promised rain tomorrow
we'll be able to breathe clean air.

עין הדרקון

כְּשֶׁהָרוּחַ חוֹדֶרֶת
אֶל חֵיק הָעֵשֶׂב
הַדְּרָקוֹן בָּאִי קוֹמוֹדוֹ
שׁוֹמֵעַ מוּזִיקָה.
דִּמְעָה עוֹמֶדֶת בְּעֵינוֹ
לִפְנֵי שֶׁהוּא גּוֹמֵר
לִטְרֹף אֶת הָאַיָּל.

מָה עוֹשָׂה הַמּוּזִיקָה וּמָה אֵינָהּ עוֹשָׂה.
מְצַיֶּרֶת צְבָעִים בִּלְתִּי נִרְאִים
מְזַגֶּגֶת טוֹרֵף וְנִטְרָף
מְשַׁלֶּבֶת יֹפִי בְּכִעוּר, מְלַטֶּפֶת אֶת הַשְּׁתִיקָה.
מַעֲלָה דִּמְעָה בְּעֵין דְּרָקוֹן
וְשׁוֹבֶרֶת אֶת חֲנִית גְּרֶגּוֹרְיוּס הַקָּדוֹשׁ.

# EYE OF THE DRAGON

When the wind cuts
through the grass
the dragon on Komodo Island
hears music.
A tear lingers in his eye
just before he finishes
mauling the deer.

What music can and cannot do.
It paints invisible colors
mates prey with predator
mixes beauty with ugliness, caresses silence.
It brings a tear to the eye of a dragon
and shatters St. George's spear.

מה שחומק

מַה שֶּׁחוֹמֵק מִשְּׁמוֹ
מַה שֶּׁמוֹחֵק אֶת צַלְמֵנוּ
מַה שֶׁאִי אֶפְשָׁר שֶׁיִּהְיֶה, וְהָיָה
מַה שֶּׁלֹּא נִתָּן לְהָקִיא וְלֹא לִבְלֹעַ
הוּא צֵל לָבָן הַמּוּנָח עַל כָּל מִלָּה.

עוֹרְבָן צָעִיר חוֹצֶה בָּאֲלַכְסוֹן
עֵץ הַתּוּת מוֹשִׁיט אֶת עָלָיו הַגְּדוֹלִים לַחַלּוֹנִי
בֵּינֵיהֶם תָּר כָּרוּחַ צְחוֹק יְלָדִים.

## WHAT EVADES

What evades its name
what erases our image
what couldn't have been, and was
what can't be spewed out nor swallowed
is a white shadow resting on every word.

A young jaybird crosses by diagonally
the berry tree extends its large leaves toward my window
between them, children's laughter explores
like the wind.

## לא סקילה וכריבדיס

בְּשַׁחַר נְעוּרַי אֵלֵי יָוָן וַעֲלִילוֹתֵיהֶם שֶׁל גִּבּוֹרֶיהָ
הָיוּ לִי מוּחָשִׁיִּים מִכַּמָּה וְכַמָּה דְּמֻיּוֹת שֶׁל יוֹמְיוֹמִי.
אֲבָל הַפַּעַם לֹא סְקִילָה וְכָרִיבְדִיס, רַק גֶּשֶׁם זִלְעָפוֹת
וְשִׁטָּפוֹן עָצוּם מָנְעוּ כָּל תַּחְבּוּרָה בַּיְצִיאָה מִנְּמַל הַתְּעוּפָה
שֶׁל בְּרָטִיסְלָבָה, שֶׁאֵינִי יוֹדֵעַ מַדּוּעַ אֲנִי שָׁב אֵלֶיהָ בִּמְקוֹם לְהֵרָדֵם.
כְּבָר מְאֻחָר.
הַאִם שָׁכַחְתִּי שֶׁעִיר זוֹ הֵקִיאָה אוֹתִי מִתּוֹכָהּ וְהִשְׁאִירָה חֲסַר אוֹנִים
כְּמוֹ טוֹבֵעַ תַּחַת שָׁמֵי נְחֹשֶׁת?
הַאִם לְהוֹדוֹת לָהּ, כִּי – בְּהָפוּךְ עַל הָפוּךְ – אוֹתִי הִצִּילָה?
הַסִּירֵנוֹת בִּכְבִישׁ בֵּית שְׁאָן נִבְלָעוֹת בָּרַעַשׁ הֶעָמוּם שֶׁל רַכֶּבֶת הָעֵמֶק.
אֲנִי מְגַשֵּׁשׁ לְעֵבֶר הַשָּׁעוֹן וְאֵינִי מוֹצֵא.
יֵשׁ וְהַזִּכָּרוֹן מַרְעִיל כְּמוֹ אַרְסָן שֶׁמֵּמִית לְאַט.
אֲנִי עָיֵף, עָיֵף מְאֹד.
לֹא קִיקְלוֹף חוֹסֵם אֶת הַכְּנִיסָה לִרְחוֹב גְּרֶסְלִינְג וְלֹא נוֹתֵן לִי לְהַגִּיעַ לְבֵית נְעוּרַי.
אֵיפֹה אֲנִי?
אֲנִי שׁוֹמֵעַ מַשֶּׁהוּ. שׁוֹמֵעַ נְכוֹחָה?
"לֹא פֶּנֶלוֹפֶּה מַמְתִּינָה לְךָ. פֶּרְסֶפוֹנֶה."

# NOT SCYLLA AND CHARYBDIS

In my early youth it was the Greek gods and the deeds of their heroes
who were more real to me than figures of my daily life.
But this time it's not Scylla and Charybdis, only torrential rain
and a great flood preventing all transportation from exiting the airport
of Bratislava, where I don't know why I've returned instead of falling asleep.
It's already late.
Have I forgotten how that city spewed me out and left me helpless
like someone drowning under a brass sky?
Should I thank it, because – in the world turned upside down – it saved me?
The sirens on the Beit She'an road are swallowed by the dim noise of the
    valley train.
I grope for my watch and can't find it.
There are times when memory poisons like a slow-killing arsenic.
I am tired, very tired.
It isn't a Cyclops blocking the entrance to Grossling Street that prevents me
    from reaching my childhood home.
Where am I?
I hear something. Do I hear right?
"It's not Penelope who waits for you. It's Persephone."

מרסיאס שהתחרה עם אפולו

עם זכר פול צלאן

קְלוּף עוֹר
בְּשָׂרִי זוֹהֵר כְּמוֹ וְרָדִים שְׁחֹרִים.

הֵי נְהִי, הָאַוּלוֹס, צֶמֶד חֲלִילִים
עַד מָה חֲסַר אוֹנִים לְהַבִּיעַ,
וְלוּ בְּצֵל שֶׁל צְלִיל, לָמָה
נְטוּל פְּנֵי אֱנוֹשׁ מְסֻגָּל.

בַּשֶּׁמֶשׁ הַלּוֹהֶטֶת קַר לִי.
אָנוּס אוֹר לְאַט לְאַט אֲנִי זוֹכֵר:
מַרְסִיאָס שְׁמִי.

עֵמֶק, עֵמֶק שֶׁלִּי, עַכְשָׁו נָקִד וּבָרֹד בְּצִלְלֵי עֲנָנִים
קָשֶׁה לְהִפָּרֵד מִמְּךָ.
אָמְרוּ שֶׁאַתָּה חֲלוֹם
שֶׁהַחַיִּים אֵינָם אֶלָּא חֲלוֹם
שֶׁל פַּלָּצוּת וּפֶלֶא.

# MARSYAS WHO COMPETED WITH APOLLO

*In memory of Paul Celan*


Stripped of skin
my flesh glows like black roses.

Alas, the aulos, double-reed pipe
how powerless it is to express,
and even with a shadow-note, what
one lacking in humanity is capable of.

In the burning sun I'm cold.
Light-ravished slowly slowly I remember:
My name is Marsyas.

Valley, my valley, now pied and dappled with cloud shadows
how hard it is to leave you.
They said you were a dream
that life is nothing but a dream
of shudders and wonders.

הסערה
*"We are such stuff as dreams are made on"*

עִם שְׁנֵיהֶם יַחַד,

עִם אַרְיֵאל, הָרוּחַ הַצָּלוּל, הָאַוְרִירִי,

עִם קָלִיבָּן, מַקְדִּיר פָּנִים,

עוֹזְרָהּ שֶׁל סִיקָרוֹס הַמְכַשֵּׁפָה, אִמּוֹ.

תְּזוּזָה קַלָּה וְקָלִיבָּן הוּא קָנִיבָּל, וְלֹא

יִהְיֶה עָלֶיךָ לְהַרְחִיק לִמְצֹא מִבְּנֵי מִינוֹ

עִם רֶצַח בָּעֵינַיִם וְקִלְלוֹת מָוֶת בְּפִיהֶם.

וּבַעֲלוֹת חֲלֵב הַשַּׁחַר מֵעַל אַרְיֵאל

אַחֲרֵי לֵיל סְעָרָה הַקֶּסֶם תַּם.

חֲלוֹם כְּשׁוּף הַגְּאֻלָּה, חֲלוֹם קִסְמֵי הָאִי.

הַמַּפְרִשִׂים אֶל נְסִיכוּת מִילָן – חֲלוֹם שֶׁל חֲלוֹם.

רַק חֹסֶר הַמּוֹצָא נוֹשֵׂא אֵלֵינוּ אֶת עֵינָיו הַפְּעוּרוֹת.

וּבְיוֹם בָּהִיר וְיָם שָׁלֵו אַטְלַנְטִיס תִּשְׁתַּקֵּף בַּמְּצוּלוֹת.

# THE TEMPEST

*"We are such stuff as dreams are made on"*

With both of them together,

with Ariel, the lucid spirit, the aery,

with Caliban, grim-faced,

helper of Sycorax the Witch, his mother.

A slight shift and Caliban becomes Cannibal, you

won't have far to go to find his kind

with murder in their eyes and death-curses in their mouths.

And as the milk of dawn rises over Ariel

after a stormy night, the magic ends.

Dream of redemption's sorcery, dream of the island's magic.

The sails of Milan's dukedom – a dream of dreams.

Only the no-exit stares at us with its wide eyes.

And on a clear day with a calm sea, one can see Atlantis in the depths.

רעב

אֲנִי רָעֵב רָעֵב רָעֵב עַד־לֹא־אֵדַע כַּמָּה רָעֵב.
בֵּין קִרְקוּר לְקִרְקוּר שֶׁל בִּטְנִי אֲנִי נִזְכָּר
שֶׁמִּישֶׁהוּ אָכַל גַּם כָּל מַה שֶּׁנָּשַׁר מִשֻּׁלְחָנוֹ, שֶׁכָּרַע עַל בִּרְכָּיו
לֶאֱסֹף אֶת כָּל הַפֵּרוּרִים
עַד שֶׁשָּׁכַח לְהָסֵב לַשֻּׁלְחָן
צַלַּחְתּוֹ נִשְׁאֲרָה רֵיקָה
הוּא הָפַךְ לְאָמָּן הָרָעָב.
שָׁמַעְתִּי זֹאת? קָרָאתִי זֹאת?
הֵיכָן וּמָתַי בַּבִּלְבּוּל הַכְּלָלִי הַזֶּה
כְּשֶׁהָרָעָב שֶׁלִּי אֵינְסוֹפִי.

# HUNGRY

I'm hungry hungry hungry past-rhyme-or-reason hungry.
From growl to growl of my belly I remember
someone who ate everything that fell from his table, he got down on his
    knees
to collect all the crumbs
until he forgot to return to the table
his plate remained empty
he had become a hunger artist.
Did I hear that? Did I read it?
Where and when in this general confusion
with my hunger that is endless.

הַשַּׁעַר פָּתוּחַ אֲבָל אֵין כְּנִיסָה.
הַלַּיְלָה יוֹרֵד כִּמְעַט בְּחָפְזָה כְּדַרְכּוֹ בִּמְקוֹמוֹתֵינוּ
וְאֵיפֹה אַנִּיחַ אֶת רֹאשִׁי?
לֹא דַאֲגָתֵנוּ, אוֹמֵר מִישֶׁהוּ.
אֲבָל לֹא מִדַּעְתִּי בָּאתִי לְכָאן.
יֵשׁ טָעֲוֹת? אַתָּה קוֹבֵל? – אוֹתוֹ הַקּוֹל
אוֹ אַחֵר.
אֵין. לֹא, מְמַלְמְלוֹת שְׂפָתַי.
אָז לֵךְ לְךָ.
אֲבָל קָרָה וְאוּלַי קוֹרֶה שֶׁיֵּשׁ גַּם רִגְעֵי אֹשֶׁר, אֲנִי לוֹחֵשׁ.
בַּעַל הָאֲחֻזָּה הוּא שֶׁאוֹסֵר כְּנִיסָה?
אֵיזֶה בַּעַל הָאֲחֻזָּה? אַתָּה צוֹחֵק? צוֹחֵק לִי בַּפָּנִים?
וְלָמָּה נֶעֶלְמוּ רַבִּים כָּל כָּךְ?
לֹא עַל כָּל שְׁאֵלָה יֵשׁ תְּשׁוּבָה, מְצַרְצְרִים
אֵינְסוֹף צְרָצְרִים בְּצִרְצוּר מַחֲרִישׁ אָזְנַיִם.
הַאִם אֵין כָּאן מִי שֶׁאַחֲרַאי בֶּאֱמֶת? מִתְאַלֵּם קוֹלִי.

בֶּאֱמֶת בֶּאֱמֶת בֶּאֱמֶת חוֹזֵר הֶהָד.

# THE ECHO

The gate is open but there's no entering.

Night descends almost hastily, as it does in our regions

and where will I rest my head?

*Not our worry,* someone says.

But I arrived here unintentionally.

*You have grievances? You're complaining?* – the same voice

or another.

None. No, my lips murmur.

*Then get thee out.*

But it happened and maybe happens that there are also moments of joy, I
    whisper.

Is it the estate owner who forbids entry?

*What estate owner? Are you laughing? Laughing in my face?*

And why have so many disappeared?

Not every question has an answer, the endless

crickets chirp in their deafening chirping.

Isn't there anyone here who's really in charge? My voice becomes mute.

*Really really really,* the Echo keeps repeating.

מילים

הַמִּלִּים שֶׁלֹּא נֶאֶמְרוּ
דּוֹפְקוֹת עַל דֶּלֶת
הַלֵּב הַפּוֹחֵד.

עוֹנֶה הַהֵד:

לְךָ דוּמִיָּה תְּהִלָּה.

## WORDS

The words that weren't spoken
are knocking on the door
of the frightened heart.

The Echo answers:

Silence for you is praise.

הֱיוּ שלום, תודה


הֱיוּ שָׁלוֹם, תּוֹדָה
כִּי בָּאתֶם. מַה
חַיֵּי אָדָם לְבַדָּם
עִם לִבּוֹ הָרַע
עִם לִבּוֹ הַטַּך, עִם עֵינָיו הַסְּתוּרוֹת
נְשׁוֹחֵחַ קִמְעָה, נִחְיֶה
כְּמוֹ בָּאַגָּדָה, נַחֲלִיף
מִלִּים סְפוּרוֹת, נֹאמַר
שָׁלוֹם, שָׁלוֹם
הַמַּיִם הַפּוֹרְחִים. הַלֶּחֶם הַשָּׁלֵם.
כֵּן. הָיִיתִי. כָּאן. כֻּלָּנוּ. כֵּן
תּוֹדָה.

## FAREWELL TO YOU, THANK YOU

Farewell to you, thank you
for coming. What
is a person's life on its own
with his wicked heart
with his humble heart, with his wild eyes
we'll talk a bit, we'll live
like in the fairy tale, we'll exchange
a few words, we'll say
Hello, Farewell
Shalom, shalom
The budding waters. The unbroken bread.
Yes. I existed. Here. All of us. Yes
Thank you.

# NOTES

"Old Man in Love," chosen for this collection's epigraph text, is from Ruebner's collection *Still Before* (2017). Lines 9–14 reference the action of the Passover Haggadah song *Chad Gadya* – "One Kid Goat" – which traditionally ends the Passover Seder. The italicized words are directly from the song, the first two in Aramaic (the dominant language of the song) and the last in Hebrew. Words have been added or changed in the English rendering of the poem in order to adhere to the rhyming couplets of the original Hebrew (which appears at the end of this Notes section). The single line which deviates from this rhyming couplet pattern is line 14 in the original, recreated in line 15 of the English translation.

Biblical citations in these notes are from the Jewish Publication Society (JPS) translation, unless otherwise indicated.

## I / THE CROSSROADS

*The Crossroads* (פרשת הדרכים) was published in 2015, two years after the collection Ruebner declared as his last and hence titled *Last Ones* (אחרונים). The poems included here represent approximately a third of the poems in the collection.

In March 2015, a selection of Ruebner's kibbutz photographs was shown in an exhibit also titled *The Crossroads*, curated by Guy Raz. The catalogue of the exhibit was published in 2017 under the title *Tuvia Ruebner: A Doubled Gaze* (טוביה ריבנר: מבט כפול).

### HAYDN

For a video clip of Ruebner reading this poem, see https://vimeo.com /388794102. The clip is from Omri Lior's film on Ruebner, titled "Poems from the Depth of the Field." For a 5-minute video collage of pieces from Lior's film, see https://www.wordswithaview.com/tuvia-ruebner

### A PLENTITUDE OF FLOWERS

LINE 10: The Hebrew word for language, *lashon*, means also tongue (literal). Hence, this line reads also as "The tongue cannot achieve the taste of color."

LINES 12–13, 17: The addressee of the opening imperatives is male, as are the "you" and "your" in the lines that follow.

### WRITING POEMS

LINE 18: The word החטיא – rendered as "missed the mark" – denotes also "to cause [another] to sin."

23.2.2014

LINE 1: Ruebner is referencing here his close friends and colleagues Dan Pagis (Israeli writer and Holocaust survivor, 1930–1986), Ozer Rabin (Israeli poet, 1921–1999) and Yaakov (Yankele) Shabtai (Israeli novelist and playwright, 1934–1981).

LINE 3: The Hebrew word ונצרם, here rendered as "packed them up," might be rendered also as "bound them up," and evokes the following verse from the prayer for the dead, El Malei Rahamim: וְיִצְרֹר בִּצְרוֹר הַחַיִּים אֶת נִשְׁמָתוֹ – "[May God] bind up the soul [of the departed] in the bonds of life...." Jewish tombstones often have etched on them the acronym תנצב"ה – תְּהֵא נִשְׁמָתוֹ/ה צְרוּרָה בִּצְרוֹר הַחַיִּים – "May his/her soul be bound up in the bonds of life."

LINE 6: The Hebrew phrase *bigufam habahir*, rendered here as "in their bright body," coupled with the phoenix image, may be evoking the mystical work *Sefer HaBahir* and its opening verse: וְעַתָּה לֹא רָאוּ אוֹר בָּהִיר הוּא בַּשְּׁחָקִים וְרוּחַ עָבְרָה וַתְּטַהֲרֵם – "Now one cannot see the sun, though it be bright in the heavens, until the wind comes and clears it [of clouds]" ( Job 37:21; NJPS).

LINE 7: The quoted line is Ruebner's epigraph to his poem "Why Shashtin," in his collection *Last Ones*, p. 37. The full epigraph reads as follows: "Because pain is pulled to the wound and the wound is pulled to the pain. / Because nothing is closer to your heart than what has been lost, and more beloved than the one who is gone."

LINE 13: Cf. Proverbs 14:15. Also, the "believes" of line's opening – *ma'amin* / מַאֲמִין – is echoed in the nurse's name – Emunah / אֱמוּנָה – as both words are of the same א מ נ root.

LINE 14: The reference is to the bus accident in 1950 in which Ada Ruebner (née Klein), Ruebner's first wife, was killed and Ruebner was seriously wounded. Ruebner suffered from burns over much of his body. See the description of the accident in the poem "What Can We Say to the Dead," pp. 22–23.

FINAL LINE: Literally, "your images illuminate my eyelids' inside...."

## [THE SILENCE]

FINAL LINE: The Hebrew phrase *al penei ha-* / עַל־פְּנֵי הַ־ / "over the face of the" – rendered here more colloquially as "over the" – evokes the second verse of the book of Genesis: "Now the earth was unformed and void, and darkness was upon **the face of** the deep [עַל־פְּנֵי תְהוֹם] and the spirit of God hovered over **the face of** the waters [עַל־פְּנֵי הַמָּיִם]." In the biblical narrative, this is the liminal moment before the Creation begins.

## ALMOST MY BROTHER

EPIGRAPH: D.P. is Dan Pagis, Ruebner's closest friend. For an earlier poem to Pagis, first published in Ruebner's 1990 collection *And He Hastenth to His Place*, see "Farewell from a Friend," *In the Illuminated Dark*, pp. 92–93.

LINE 1: Sanhedria is the name of a Jewish cemetery adjacent to the ultra-orthodox neighborhood of Sanhedria in Jerusalem.

LINE 4: In Israel, the dead are traditionally not buried in a coffin. The body, wrapped in shrouds, is covered with a *tallit* – a prayer shawl – during the eulogies and prayer service. The general contours of the body are visible.

LINE 8: Ruebner uses the English word "dignity," transliterated into Hebrew.

LINE 9: In a personal communication on March 30th 2019, Ruebner glossed this line by explaining that after the death camps, Pagis doubted whether he was in fact alive at all.

LINE 16: Kibbutz Merchavia in the Jezreel Valley, where Ruebner lived for almost eight decades.

## WHAT CAN WE SAY TO THE DEAD

EPIGRAPH: Ada Ruebner (née Klein) and Tuvia Ruebner married in 1944; in August 1949, their daughter Miriam (known as Miriyami) was born. In February 1950, on their first trip away from the kibbutz after the birth of their daughter, the Ruebners were involved in a bus accident; Ada was killed in the accident. She was 25 years old.

LINE 24: Literally, "May your dust clods be sweet," a traditional expression spoken to, or about (with third-person possessive pronoun), the dead.

## BEFORE FIRST MORNING TWILIGHT

LINE 4: The Hebrew rendered here as "murmur" – *hemiyah* – means soft sounds, such as animals might make, for example cooing or purring. In archaic usage, the word also signifies longing.

LINE 5: Cf. Genesis 3:9: "And the Lord God called unto the man, and said unto him: 'Where art thou?' [אַיֶּכָּה]." For הִנֵּנִי ("Here am I"), of the many examples of biblical characters answering a call thus, perhaps the most resonant example is Moses answering God who speaks to him from out of the burning bush. Cf. Exodus 3: 4: "… God called unto him out of the midst of the bush, and said: 'Moses, Moses.' And he said: 'Here am I [הִנֵּנִי].'"

## LAMPEDUSA: TERRA FERMÉ

The footnote, a translation of Ruebner's original Hebrew footnote, appears thus at the bottom of the poem in the collection *The Crossroads*.

## SURPRISES

LINE 10: The line's first word, *demut* – form or likeness – evokes Genesis 1:26: "And God said: 'Let us make man in our image, after our likeness…'" – וַיֹּאמֶר אֱלֹהִים, נַעֲשֶׂה אָדָם בְּצַלְמֵנוּ כִּדְמוּתֵנוּ. The word "human" has been added to recreate in the English that evocation.

LINE 16: The adage referenced is from *Sefer ben Sira*, Haggigah Tractate 13a. The entire verse is: "Of the more wondrous than you, make no query; of the hidden from you, seek nothing." The verse appears earlier in Midrash Genesis Rabbah 8:2 in the following more expansive articulation: "Rabbi Elazar said in Bar Sira's name: 'About what is too great for thee inquire not; what is too hard for thee investigate not; about what is too wonderful for thee know not; of what is hidden from thee ask not; study what was permitted thee; thou hast no business with hidden things'" – רבי אלעזר בשם בן סירא אמר בְּגָדוֹל מִמְּךָ אַל תִּדְרֹשׁ, בְּחָזָק מִמְּךָ בַּל תַּחְקֹר, בְּמִפְלָא מִמְּךָ בַּל תֵּדַע, בִּמְכֻסֶּה מִמְּךָ אַל תִּשְׁאַל, בַּמֶּה שֶׁהֻרְשֵׁיתָ הִתְבּוֹנֵן, וְאֵין לְךָ עֵסֶק בְּנִסְתָּרוֹת.

## THE CELLAR

Ruebner's grandparents lived in the town of Shastin, Slovakia. Ruebner and his little sister Litzi would spend a month at the grandparents' home every summer. The town is now known as Šaštín-Stráže.

## SINCE THEN

LINES 15–16, 30–32: The changes to the line-breaks have been made in order to adhere as closely as possible to the lengths of the lines in the original.

## THE PERFECT WASN'T

LINE 12: The close friend being referenced is Imre Kertész (1929–2016), Jewish Hungarian author, Holocaust survivor, and winner of the Nobel Prize in Literature in 2002.

## LITANY

TITLE: *Tehinot*, literally "supplications" or "entreaties." The elevated and religious register of the word evokes sacred circumstances and holy days. The term, specifically in the Yiddish pronunciation *tkines*, references a tradition of Jewish women's private prayers and devotional texts (written in Yiddish). Additions to and deviations from the Hebrew have been made in order to render end-rhymes (slant or full), in adherence to the Hebrew original.

## PLAIN AND UNADORNED

TITLE AND LINE 1: Literally, "Not blue and not dark red" or "Without eye-shadow or rouge." The idiom originates in the Talmud, Tractate Ketubbot 17a, where a bride is praised for her natural and unadorned beauty.

LINE 6: Cf. Genesis 3:14: "And the LORD God said unto the serpent: 'Because thou hast done this, cursed art thou from among all cattle, and from among all beasts of the field; upon thy belly [עַל־גְּחֹנְךָ] thou shalt thou go, and dust shalt thou eat all the days of thy life.'"

## AFTER BECKETT

Penned in the late summer of 2013, this poem was published in its English rendering before it was published in Hebrew. As per Ruebner's request, it was included in *In the Illuminated Dark*, where it appears as the book's coda poem (pp. 320–24). Its first Hebrew publication is in *The Crossroads* collection, as the book's penultimate poem.

The version in *The Crossroads* as rendered here is slightly different from the version published in *In the Illuminated Dark*. The one significant change is line 11, which does not appear in the 2013 version.

---

## II / STILL BEFORE

*Still Before* (עוד לפני) was published in 2017; all the poems in the collection were written in a single year, 2016–2017. The poems included here in English translations represent approximately half of the poems in the collection.

The book opens with the following epigraph: "One more ember of words / before the ashes" – "עוד גחלת מלים / לפני האפר"

## ANGEL BECOMING

Angels are a steady presence in Ruebner's oeuvre. See in particular his ekphrastic series "Paul Klee's Angels: Eight Drawings and One Watercolor" and "Angelus Novus" in *In the Illuminated Dark*, pp. 117–23.

## IN THE LAND OF THE DEER

TITLE: The "Land of the Deer" (plural) of the poem's title alludes to a Hebrew epithet for the land of Israel, *Eretz HaTzvi* – "Land of the Deer" (singular). Cf. Daniel 11: 42 for the single biblical usage of this epithet.

LINES 4–5: "the Valley / it's a dream" alludes to a short Hebrew folk song, written by S. Shalom, put to music by Moshe Rappaport, and first recorded in 1963. The valley referenced is Jezreel Valley. Kibbutz Merchavia, where Ruebner lived since arriving in Israel in 1941, is in the Jezreel Valley.

LINE 7: January 30th is Ruebner's birthday. In 2016, he marked his 92nd birthday.

LINES 15–16: Kochav HaYarden (Hebrew for "Star of the Jordan") is a national park on a hilltop just south of the Sea of Galilee, where the ruins of the Crusader fortress Belvoir stand. Until 1948, the Palestinian village of Kawkab al-Hawa (Arabic for "Star of the Wind") existed in and around the fortress ruins. The Palestinian village of Kawkab al-Hawa was depopulated in the battles of May 1948, and was destroyed in September that same year. Ruebner provides both the Hebrew and Arabic names for the site.

An additional line was added to the English rendering in order to accommodate the Hebrew, Arabic, and English names of this site, without deviating from the lines' length.

LINE 22: Cf. Psalms 132:1: "Out of the depths have I called Thee, Lord."

## [WRITING A POEM TODAY IS]

In 2016, Ruebner began writing haikus, adhering strictly to the 17-syllable format. Some of these haikus were included in the *Still Before* collection. In 2018, Ruebner published a collection titled *Seventeen*, devoted exclusively to these haikus. This poem was republished in the 2018 collection.

The syllabic count of the Hebrew lines is 5/7/5.

## THE VALLEY TRAIN, AN AUTUMN FAIRY TALE

The valley of the title and the poem is the Jezreel Valley, south of the Lower Galilee. The original train through the Jezreel Valley, known as The Valley Train (רַכֶּבֶת הָעֵמֶק), and operating until 1948, was known for its great slowness; hence, the tall-tales that were told about its snail's pace. In 2011, Israel Railways began refurbishing and reconstructing the long-dormant and dismantled Valley Train, and in 2016, the line reopened. On October 6th, 2016, the older citizens of the Jezreel Valley were invited to travel together, as guests of the railway, on one of the reinstated line's maiden voyages. Ruebner and his wife Galila were among the travelers. Ruebner includes the date on the original poem.

LINE 7: "the valley is a dream" is again a reference to the short folk song alluded to in "In the Land of the Deer." The song's title is also its refrain.

LINE 13: "From Beit Alfa to Nahalal" is a repeated line in the Hebrew folk song "Song of the Valley" (*Shir HaEmek*), words written by Natan Alterman and music by Daniel Samborski. Beit Alfa (a kibbutz) and Nahalal (a moshav) were both founded in the early 1920s and signify the pioneer era in Israeli history.

LINE 28: This line begins a new stanza.

LINE 31: The word rendered here as "throng" – *ambuha* – is from Aramaic and is not part of colloquial speech.

LINE 32: Beit Yehoshua is a moshav in central Israel with an active railway station.

## NO WAY

The period from October 2015 through October 2016 became known in Israel as the "Knife Intifada," due to the preponderance of stabbings perpetrated by Palestinians against individual Israelis. Many of the stabbers were very young men and women.

LINE 1: Moloch, or Molech in the Hebrew, was a Canaanite deity associated with child sacrifice. For example, cf. 2 Kings 23:10: "And he defiled Topheth, which is in the valley of the sons of Hinnom, that no one might burn his son or his daughter as an offering to Molech."

LINES 6–8: The allusion is to American novelist and poet Gertrude Stein (1874–1946), who made her home in Paris from 1903 until the end of her life.

LINES 11–13: On October 18th, 2015, a Israeli Bedouin entered the Beer Sheva bus station, shot and killed the guard at the entrance, fired additional bullets into the crowd, and was then shot and killed by security personnel. An Eritrean refugee bystander named Haftom Zarhum was mistaken by security forces as a second shooter. Zarhum was shot six times by the security forces and beaten by civilian bystanders as he lay on the ground wounded. Zarhum died of his injuries. The lynching of Zarhum was caught on camera and shown on the evening news.

LINE 16: Shu'afat is an Arab neighborhood in East Jerusalem. Large portions of the lands belonging to Shu'afat (once a town) have been confiscated for the expansion of Jewish neighborhoods in the area.

## GAZA NIGHTMARE

TITLE: The Hebrew title is only "Nightmare," but the Israeli reader will easily identify the "nightmare" of the poem as referring to one of the many retaliatory Israeli air-strikes on Gaza. Hence, the word "Gaza" has been added to the English to effect a similar identification and understanding in the English reader. The Hebrew collocation for "nightmare" – *halom balahot* – literally means "a dream of terrors."

## VAYIKRAH

TITLE: *VaYikrah* is the third book of the five books of Moses, known as Leviticus in English. As with all five books of Moses, the book's name is the first, or one of the first, words in the book's opening verse. Leviticus opens thus: *Va'yikrah el Moshe, va'yidaber Adonai eilav* – "And God called to Moses and spoke to him..." – וַיִּקְרָא, אֶל־מֹשֶׁה; וַיְדַבֵּר יְהוָה אֵלָיו, מֵאֹהֶל מוֹעֵד לֵאמֹר *VaYikrah* is also the name of the 24th weekly Torah portion in the yearly cycle, and includes Leviticus 1:1–5:26.

## 1 *VAYIKRAH* (AND HE CALLED)

LINE 1: The first denotation of *tsara'at* (צרעת) is leprosy, though figuratively it signifies any plague. The two words of this opening line – *tsa'ar hatsara'at* – achieve a strong sound pattern with the repeated tsaddi and the six-times repeated "ah" vowel sound. In the English rendering, I've chosen "anguish" for the word *tsa'ar* – more commonly translated as "sorrow" – in order to compensate for that lost sound pattern with the strong assonance of "plague" and "anguish."

LINE 10: *einda'at* is a neologism, a combination of *ein* (not) and *da'at* (knowledge or wisdom). The new compound word may be read as a truncated version of the idiom אין להעלותו על הדעת – "that's inconceivable."

## 2 *KORBAN* (SACRIFICE)

The word *korban* – meaning sacrifice or offering – appears in the Bible for the first time in the second verse of Leviticus. As the laws of ritual sacrifice are the focus of this chapter and the ones to follow, the word *korban* is then repeated many times. While the poem is referencing the biblical denotation of the word and is evoking the biblical chapters of Leviticus on the rules of animal sacrifice, it is also using the word *korban* in its modern usage as "victim." See Ruebner's poem *Korban Vishuv* ("Victim, Again") in *In the Illuminated Dark*, pp. 176–77. Who the *korban* is in this poem is not stipulated; however, the context of the Leviticus laws stating that the sacrifice must be תָּמִים – "unblemished" or "innocent" – and most often male, may lead one to read this sacrifice as a young male soldier.

The "no" and "not" of the English rendering are the same one word in the Hebrew – *lo*. Thus, this *lo* appears anaphorically seven times in the poem

LINE 5: The word *kri'at* is the construct form of the word *kri'ah* / קריעה – which refers to the ritual rending of one's garment at the graveside as an act of mourning. The word also evokes its near-homophone, *kri'ah* / קריאָה – which means both "calling out" and "reading."

LINE 8: For the adjective *hazaruk* ("the cast off"), see the verb *zarku* ("they threw") in Leviticus 1:5, 1:11, 3:2, 3:8 and 3:13. Five times the sons of Aaron – the Priests – are described "casting off" or "dashing" – *vezarku* / וְזָרְקוּ – the blood of the sacrificed animals around the altar. For example, see Leviticus 3:2: "And he shall lay his hand upon the head of his offering, and kill it at the door of the tent of meeting; and Aaron's sons the priests shall dash the blood against the altar round about."

## 3 GOLD

LINE 7: There is a tradition with roots in the Amoraic midrashim that reads the word *egel* / עגל (calf) as an acronym for various sins ascribed to the Israelites, beyond idolatry. The first letter of *egel* – ע – is said to connote sexual misconduct, *aryot* / עריות. The other letters are associated with *gezel* / גזל (robbery) and *lashon harah* / לשון הרע (slander).

LINES 8–9: Cf. Psalms 114: 4: הֶהָרִים, רָקְדוּ כְאֵילִים; גְּבָעוֹת, כִּבְנֵי-צֹאן – "The mountains skipped [danced] like rams, the hills like young sheep."

LINE 14: The cherubim, a type of angel-figure, are first mentioned in Genesis 3:24, in the final verse of the expulsion from the Garden of Eden narrative. They were apparently tasked, together with the "flaming sword," with preventing Adam and Eve from reentering the garden: "So He drove out the man; and He placed at the east of the Garden of Eden the cherubim, and the flaming sword which turned every way, to keep the way to the tree of life."

The cherubim are reintroduced in Exodus 25, during the desert sojourn, when Moses is given instructions how to construct the desert sanctuary (*mishkan*). In this description, two carefully crafted cherubim of gold are to be placed on the ark-cover (*parochet*), facing each other (וּפְנֵיהֶם אִישׁ אֶל-אָחִיו), their wings extended toward the other though apparently not touching (25:18–20). It is there, in the space between the two angels' extended wings, that God promises he will meet with Moses: "And there I will meet with thee, and I will speak with thee from above the ark-cover, from between the two cherubim which are upon the Ark of the Testimony…" (25:22).

## WONDERINGS

Israeli artist Yosl Bergner (1920–2017) was born in Austria, grew up in Warsaw, Poland, and immigrated to Australia in 1937. He lived in Australia until 1948, when he moved to Israel. Bergner and Ruebner were lifelong friends. For an earlier poem to Bergner, see "Yosl, Yosl" in *In the Illuminated Dark*, pp. 246–47.

## AMEN

The second stanza refrain is referencing the Passover Haggadah song "Dayenu," recounting one by one God's gifts to the Jewish people, starting with the redemption from slavery and ending with building the Temple. Each line ends with the refrain *dayenu* – "[that gift] would have been enough [for us]."

LINE 13: The line references a verse from the *Shema* prayer – "These words, which I command you today, shall be upon your heart … when you rise and when you lie down [וּבְשָׁכְבְּךָ וּבְקוּמֶךָ]." The singular "you" of the prayer (and biblical verse) has been made plural. Cf. Deuteronomy 6:4–9.

LINE 15: Literally, "by tooth and eye," meaning to have emerged from a conflict having suffered significant losses. The origin of the idiom is in biblical laws, which evolved from Ancient Near Eastern Law Codes, regarding the appropriate treatment of one's servant. If the master causes his servant to lose an eye or a tooth, he must set that servant free. Cf. Exodus 21: 26–27: "When a man strikes the eye of his slave, male or female, and destroys it, he shall let him go free on account of his eye. If he knocks out the tooth of his slave, male or female, he shall let him go free on account of his tooth" (NJPS).

## A BOY

LINES 6–7: The line-break here is different from the Hebrew in order to maintain the original's line-lengths.

LINE 8: The line alludes to, and rewrites, the fourth line of the popular Jewish liturgical song *Adon Olam*: "He was and he is, he will be in glory."

## DURING THE DAYS OF AWE

TITLE: Literally, "Between the new moon [or New Year] and the tenth day [or Day of Judgment]." The word used here for new moon – *keseh* / כֶּסֶה – is from the כ ס ה root, meaning to conceal or be concealed, referencing the new moon's invisibility. There are, however, those who read *keseh* as indicating the full moon, the fifteenth of the month – Cf. Psalms 81: 4: "Blow the shofar on the new moon, on the full moon [*keseh*] for our feast-day." The Days of Awe, the appellation given to the ten days between Rosh Hashanah and Yom Kippur, are considered days of particular holiness, designated for repentance and readying oneself for the Day of Atonement.

The sections in this poem, each a seventeen-syllable haiku, were republished in Ruebner's 2018 haiku collection *Seventeen* as discrete poems, each on a separate page and untitled. Changes have been inserted into the English renderings when needed to hold to the seventeen-syllable format.

## ECUADOR

LINE 19: The reference is to Benjamin, Jacob's youngest son; he and Joseph were the two sons born to Rachel. In the biblical narrative, after Joseph is thought dead, Jacob keeps Benjamin close to him, fearing for his safety and well-being. See Genesis 42–43. It is in this narrative, and specifically in relationship to Jacob's fear of losing Benjamin, that the word *shechol* – bereavement, specifically of a child – is first introduced in the Bible. See Genesis 42:36, and Genesis 43:14, where Jacob says, "...And as for me, if I be bereaved [of my children], I am bereaved."

Ruebner's second son, Moran, disappeared in Ecuador while traveling there in the winter of 1983. Moran was twenty-three years old at the time. No trace of him was ever found.

## [WITH THE BLACK PIT]

LINE 6: The New Testament parable of "The Prodigal Son" is known in Hebrew as "The Lost Son" – *ha-ben ha-oved*. The biblical lost son returns; Ruebner's does not.

Cf. Luke 15:11–32, in particular 23–24: "And bring the fatted calf here and kill it and let us eat and be merry; for this my son was dead and is alive again; he was lost and is found" (NKJV). See also Lea Goldberg's poem cycle "Ha-ben Ha-oved."

## THERE ARE SHOUTS

LINE 9: *Ja'hannam*, as Ruebner has it in the original Hebrew poem, is Arabic for "hell," a cognate with the Hebrew word *gehinnom*. The Hebrew word originated in the Jerusalem place name Gei-Hinnom, "Valley of Hinnom" or sometimes known as Gei Ben-Hinnom, "Valley of the son of Hinnom." Referenced numerous times in the Bible, the place was known and cursed as a site of human sacrifice, particularly of children. The exact location of the valley is given in Joshua 15:8 and carries this name until today. The practice of the sacrifice of children in this place is described in Jeremiah 7:30–31: "... the people of Judah have done what displeases me – declares the Lord.... They have built the shrines of Topheth in the Valley of Ben-Hinnom to burn their sons and daughters in fire – which I never commanded...."

To create the same recognition in the English-language reader as the Arabic *Ja'hannan* creates in the Hebrew reader, I've added the recognizable Latin word *Infernus* to the line.

LINES 10–11: "takes me under its wings" is referencing the poem "Take Me Under Your Wing" by Haim Nahman Bialik. The first and last stanzas of Bialik's iconic poem begin with the line: "Take me under your wing" – הַכְנִיסִינִי תַּחַת כְּנָפֵךְ (a female addressee). Bialik's poem, put to music and sung by Arik Einstein, is a well-known and very popular folk song.

The alternative line-break in the English is to adhere more closely to the length of lines in the Hebrew text.

## MOTHER AND FATHER

Gazárka forest, Trnava, and Senica are all places in Slovakia, not far from Bratislava, Ruebner's hometown. Ruebner's mother was from Shashtin, and Ruebner and his sister would spend a month there every summer at their grandparents' home. Ruebner's parents and sister moved to Shastin in the summer of 1941, hoping to find safety there; it was from Shashtin that they were deported to Auschwitz in June 1942. See "A Postcard from Shashtin: Autumn Fires" in *In the Illuminated Dark*, pp. 150–51.

## PHOTOGRAPH

LINES 5–7: Ruebner's son Moran was a talented young pianist.

## WILL

LINE 2: The final poetry collection published by Chaim Gouri (1923–2018) was titled *Though I Wanted a Little More More* (2015).

LINE 3: This phrase is from the dedication page of *Though I Wanted a Little More More*, that reads thus: "For My Beloveds – Till the Edge of More." Gouri dedicates the book to his three daughters, their partners and his six grand-children, including all twelve names in the dedication.

LINE 14: A copy of Rembrandt's "Return of the Prodigal Son," a gift from a friend, hangs in Ruebner's home.

## AT THE HOUR

The "he" of the poem is not explicitly named. However, the word *mavet* – the Hebrew word for death – is gendered male.

LINE 6: The collocation of *ya'aleh veyavo* – literally "he'll rise up and come" – evokes the prayer of that name, added to morning, afternoon, and evening Amidah services on the new moon and festival days.

---

## III / MORE NO MORE

*More No More* (עוד לא עוד) was published in March 2019, a few weeks after Ruebner's ninety-fifth birthday. The enigmatic title could be rendered also as *No More More*, or *Not Yet More*. The poems included here in English trans-lations represent half of the poems in the collection. The book's dedication reads thus: "A memorial to my family murdered in Auschwitz / and to the friends of my youth, victims of the Nazis."

## FIREWORKS, A SONG IN OLD STYLE

This poem appears as the epigraph poem in the collection.

TITLE AND FINAL LINE: The title word *di-nur* – literally, "of light" – uses the Aramaic preposition for the genitive "of light." The phrase *ziquqei di-nur* connotes both the modern meaning of "fireworks" and the ancient meaning of "sparks of light."

## ON THE LONGEST DAY OF THE YEAR

LINE 6: Cf. Job 26:7: תֹּלֶה אֶרֶץ, עַל־בְּלִי־מָה – "He… suspends the earth over nothing" (NIV). בְּלִי־מָה literally means "without-something."

LINE 11: A Persian loanword originally meaning "something known," the word *ashkara,* rendered here as "for real," is contemporary Hebrew slang.

LINE 14: The phrase *haval al ha-zeman* חבל על הזמן, rendered here as "it's wild," means literally "it's a waste of time." Signaling a strong slang register, it can be used in a positive or negative sense (as in, it's a waste of time talking about it because it's so good, or so bad).

## UNDERGROUND

LINE 1: This opening line reads differently in the published collection. Ruebner changed the Hebrew in a personal communication, March 30th, 2019.

LINE 12: The line is referencing and inverting the following idiom: "Blessings are not found save in what is hidden from the eye" – אין הברכה מצויה אלא בדבר הסמוי מן העין.

## *EIKHA* / O HOW

TITLE: Literally meaning "How," *eikha* is the opening word of the Book of Lamentations and in Hebrew is the book's name. Traditionally read on the fast day of Tisha B'Av, the book laments the destruction of Jerusalem. Line 4 of the poem uses the title's *eikha* again, repeating the lamenting query.

PENULTIMATE LINE: The collocation of *ad anah,* used ten times in the Bible, reestablishes a biblical register toward the poem's end. Cf. for example Job 19:2: "How long [עַד־אָנָה] will you grieve my soul and crush me with words." Cf. also Psalms 13:2–3, where the collocation is used four times in two verses: "How long, O Lord; will you ignore me forever? How long will you hide your face from me? How long will I have cares on my mind, grief in my heart all day? How long will my enemy have the upper hand?" (NJPS).

## ALL THIS SUFFERING

An earlier version of this poem appears in Ruebner's 2009 collection *Belated Beauty,* and was included in *In the Illuminated Dark,* pp. 244–45. The most significant change to the poem is the addition of the final two lines, which are new to this version.

## DRAFT FOR AN END-OF-DAYS VISION WITHOUT A TRACE OF POETRY

The footnote appears in the original Hebrew. The documentary film *Palsar Himalaya,* literally meaning "Himlayan Elite Unit" (פלס"ר – פלוגת סיור) and released in English as "Made Like a Gun," follows eight Israeli men on their motorcycle trip around the Indian Himalayas in the summer of 2014. Of varying ages and backgrounds, having served in the military at different times, all eight are Israel Defense Forces veterans suffering from PTSD. The film was directed by Eitan Zur and Eldad Prives; Prives' own struggles with PTSD are included in the film. Besides screenings at festivals and cinematheques, the film was aired on Israeli TV (where Ruebner saw it). Coincidentally, the Himalayan journey of the eight men began on the same day as the IDF land incursion into Gaza, July 2014.

For more on the film, see: https://www.haaretz.com/israel-news/culture /movies/.premium.MAGAZINE-israeli-film-on-ptsd-gets-personal-political -1.5459537

TITLE: Cf. Daniel 10:14: "Now I am come to make thee understand what shall befall thy people in the end of days; for there is yet a vision for the days."

LINE 21: Cf. Jeremiah 31:14: "A voice is heard in Ramah, lamentation, and bitter weeping, Rachel weeping for her children; she refuses to be comforted for her children, because they are not."

LINE 24: Cf. Deut. 23:20: לֹא־תַשִּׁיךְ לְאָחִיךָ, נֶשֶׁךְ כֶּסֶף נֶשֶׁךְ אֹכֶל: נֶשֶׁךְ, כָּל־דָּבָר אֲשֶׁר יִשָּׁךְ – "You shall not deduct interest from loans to your countrymen, whether in money or food or anything else that can be deducted as interest" (NJPS).

## FRIDAY

The standard idiom for "bird of the soul" is *tsipor ha-nefesh* / ציפור הנפש. *Ofot* (variously "fowl," "chicken," "bird") *ha-nefesh* – or, *ofot nafshi* (birds of my soul) – is neologistic. Due to the shared root letters between *of* / bird and *af* / flies – ע פ – the repetition of *of* throughout the poem (*of-hu, of-he*), accentuates the birds' flight.

## MESSENGERS

LINE 3: The exhibition referenced is Yosl Bergner's 1992 "Paintings to Kafka," at the Karolinum Gallery, Prague, hosted by the Franz Kafka Society of Prague.

LINE 4: The reference is to Ottilie "Ottla" Kafka (1892–1943), the youngest of Franz Kafka's three sisters. Ottla was murdered in Auschwitz in October 1943. Her two daughters, Vera (1921–2015) and Helene (1923–2005), survived the war.

LINE 12: The Maharal – a Hebrew acronym for *Moreinu Ha-rav Loew* ("Our Teacher, Rav Loew") – refers to Rabbi Judah Loew ben Bezalel, sixteenth-century scholar, teacher and mystic. He died in 1609 and is buried in the Prague Cemetery, where his elaborate tombstone draws visitors and devotees.

LINE 14: What is rendered here as "the grassy common" – הַדֶּשֶׁא הַגָּדוֹל, literally "the great grass" – is a reference to a landscape attribute of many kibbutzim, the large open grassy area outside the once-communal dining hall. As one of the oldest members of his kibbutz Merchavia, residing in one of its first houses, Ruebner's small kibbutz home abuts on "the great grass."

LINE 16: Toyo Shibata (1911–2013) was a Japanese poet who published her first poetry collection, *Don't Lose Heart*, in 2009, when she was ninety-eight years old. Her second volume, *Hyakusai* (meaning, 100 years old), was published in June 2011. Her collections became best-sellers in Japan. The phrase "she who wrote" does not appear in the Hebrew original; it was added here to indicate Shibata's gender (evident in the Hebrew).

LINE 17: The line quoted here is from Shibata's poem titled "My Reply," which is the poet's reply to the wind enticing her to cross over to the other side, and appears with the following lineation: "I'll stay here / Just a bit longer / There are still some things / Left to do."

LINE 18: The "three" of the poem's final line resonates of the three family members murdered at Auschwitz and mourned by Ruebner throughout his life: his mother, his father and his little sister Litzi.

## HE WALKS IN THE FIELDS

The poem's title and first line evoke Lea Goldberg's iconic untitled anti-war poem known as *HaOmnam*, where the phrase "you'll walk in the field" (female you) is repeated thrice.

This poem echoes two earlier Ruebner poems: "Horse and His Rider" and "Giacometti: Walking Man." See *In the Illuminated Dark*, pp. 112–13 and pp. 252–53 respectively.

## DON'T

LINE 14: A *galabiya* is a loose-fitting robe or gown, worn by men and women both. For many years, Ruebner wore white *galabiyas* through the long summer months.

LINE 15: Re: Kafka's short story "The Hunter Gracchus." In the passage alluded to, the long-dead Hunter Gracchus, explaining his situation to the burgomaster, says the following: "I had been happy to be alive and was happy to be dead. Before I came on board, I gladly threw away my rag-tag collection of guns and bags, even the hunting rifle which I had always carried so proudly, and slipped into the shroud like a young girl into her wedding dress. There I lay down and waited" (translation by Ian Johnston. From *The Kafka Project*, edited by Mauro Nervi, http://www.kafka.org/index.php).

## EYES

LINE 1: The reference is to Benjamin, Jacob's youngest son; he and Joseph were the two sons born to Rachel.

LINES 6 & 9: The order of these two lines has been inverted. What is rendered here as "at my mind and heart" appears in line 9 in the Hebrew original and reads literally, "my kidneys and my heart." The collocation of כְּלָיוֹת וָלֵב – kidneys and heart – appears several times in the Bible, usually within the context of God testing and knowing a person's deepest thoughts. For example, cf. Jeremiah 20:12: "O Lord of Hosts, you who test the righteous, who examine the heart and the mind..." (NJPS) / וַיהֹוָה צְבָאוֹת בֹּחֵן צַדִּיק רֹאֶה כְלָיוֹת וָלֵב

## NEVO

TITLE: The reference is to Mount Nevo, the mountain Moses ascends to view the Promised Land – the land he will not enter. Cf. Deuteronomy 32: 49–51 and 32:1: "And Moses went up from the plains of Moav unto Mount Nevo, to the top of Pisgah, that is over against Jericho. And the Lord showed him all the land, even Gilead as far as Dan." The Torah – the Five Books of Moses – ends with this chapter: Moses's ascension to the mountaintop, followed by his death, his burial (in an unknown place), and the people's mourning.

LINES 1–2: These two lines are an inversion of Isaiah 40:4, wherein the prophet declares that "... the rugged [הֶעָקֹב] shall be made level, and the rough places a plain [מִישׁוֹר]" – וְהָיָה הֶעָקֹב לְמִישׁוֹר. This verse appears in the chapter that begins with the words *Nahamu, nahamu* – "Comfort ye, comfort ye" – and offers redemptive images for the believers.

For an additional biblical resonance of the word *akov /* עָקֹב, see Jeremiah 17:9: "The heart is deceitful [עָקֹב] above all things, and it is exceeding weak – who can know it?" – עָקֹב הַלֵּב מִכֹּל וְאָנֻשׁ הוּא מִי יֵדָעֶנּוּ

LINES 3–4: These two lines are an inversion of and change in tense, from future-present to past, of Psalm 121:1.

## WHAT EVADES

LINE 2: Cf. Genesis 1:26: "And God said: 'Let us make man in our image, after our likeness....'" This is the single instance in the Bible of the first-person plural form of *tselem* – "our image" / צַלְמֵנוּ.

LINES 8–9: An extra line-break has been added to the poem's final line, to keep to the original's line-lengths.

## NOT SCYLLA AND CHARYBDIS

Scylla, Charybdis, and the Cyclops are among the many monster-figures which Odysseus meets during his ten-year journey home, as described in

Homer's *Odyssey*. Throughout these long years, Penelope, Odysseus's wife, faithfully awaits his return to Ithaka. Persephone, whose tale is told primarily in the Homeric "Hymn to Demeter," appears only once in the *Odyssey*. Abducted by Hades when she is a girl, Persephone becomes Queen of the Underworld.

LINE 10: Instead of the Hebrew word for "siren" – צפירה – Ruebner uses the loanword *sirenah* / סירנה – evoking thus yet another figure from the *Odyssey*, the beautiful and dangerous Sirens.

In the Hebrew collection, this poem, the three that follow, and additional poems not included here, are grouped in a section titled "Palimpsests."

## MARSYAS WHO COMPETED WITH APOLLO

Marsyas of Greek mythology – in some versions a peasant, in others a satyr – challenges the god Apollo to a musical competition, Marsyas on the double-reed flute (the aulos), Apollo on his lyre. The terms of the contest are that the winner may do with the vanquished whatever he wishes. The Muses judge the competition and determine Apollo the winner. Apollo binds Marysas to a tree and flays him alive, punishment for his hubris in challenging a god.

LINES 10–12: The reference is to the Jezreel Valley where Ruebner lived for almost eight decades.

## THE TEMPEST

The poem's title and figures refer to William Shakespeare's *The Tempest*, written and performed in 1610 or 1611, and commonly believed to be Shakespeare's last play. The poem's epigraph is spoken in the play by Prospero, the Duke of Milan. The completed passage reads as follows: "…We are such stuff / As dreams are made on, and our little life / Is rounded with a sleep" (Act 4, scene 1, 156–58).

## HUNGRY

LINE 1: *adlo'eidah* – rendered here as "past-rhyme-or-reason" – is a play on the compound word *adloyadah* / עדלאידע. The compound *adloyadah* is well known from the rabbinic directive that on the holiday of Purim one should revel and drink *ad de'lo yadah* – "until one doesn't know" (the difference between "Blessed is Mordechai" and "Cursed is Haman"). Hence, the word connotes a loss of reason and inversion of norms, due also to bacchanalian excess. The *adloyadah* refers also to the carnival-like Purim parade that takes place in many Israeli cities. Ruebner has changed the third-person past tense of *yadah* / ידע to a first-person future of *eidah* / אדע, creating thus the compound of *adlo'eidah*.

LINE 8: The allusion may be to Kafka's *Hunger Artist* (original, *Ein Hungerkünstler*).

## THE ECHO

LINE 9: Cf. Genesis 12:1, in which God instructs Abram "...Get thee out of thy country, and from thy kindred, and from thy father's house, unto the land that I will show thee."

## WORDS

FINAL LINE: These three Hebrew words are the first stich of Psalm 65:2. However, most English translations of the verse refuse the "silent" or "quiet" denotations of *dumiya* and render the stich as "Praise befits you" (NJPS) or "Praise is waiting for you" (NKJV). Perhaps these translations seek to thus avoid the apparent paradox of a Song of Praise opening with an assertion that silence does it best.

This poem appears on its own at the end of *Od Lo Od*, as a type of envoi.

---

## FAREWELL TO YOU, THANK YOU

This is the only poem in this collection not composed by Tuvia Ruebner in the final five years of his life. Ruebner published this poem in his 1967 collection *As Long As* (*Kol Od*), where it stands as that book's final text. In 2005, the poem was again chosen as a collection's final text, this time for Ruebner's selected edition *Traces of Days* (*Akevot Yamim*, edited by Rafi Weichert and Uri Hollander). Now, I follow suit, placing the poem as this book's Coda – with the sudden understanding that for more than 50 years, this gracious and generous poet was bidding us a quiet and grateful farewell.

HEBREW ORIGINAL OF THE EPIGRAPH POEM

זקן מאוהב

הַזָּקֵן אוֹהֵב, הַזָּקֵן אוֹהֵב!
גּוּפוֹ הַקּוֹפֵא לְפֶתַע לוֹהֵב.
בְּבְרוֹשׁ מִתְקַשֵּׁט בְּמִקְלַעַת קִיסוֹס הוּא רוֹאֶה צִפּוֹר.
אֶבֶן גְּדוֹלָה בְּעֵינָיו הִיא שׁוֹר.
לִדְיוּנוֹת הַחוֹל הוּא קוֹרֵא הוֹ, כַּמָּה מַיִם!
אֶחָד, הוּא טוֹעֵן, אֵינוֹ אֶלָּא שְׁנַיִם.
בְּצָהֳרֵי יָם הוּא זוֹעֵק אֵשׁ! אֵשׁ!
הוּא חוֹשֵׁשׁ, הוּא מֵעֵז, הוּא מֵעֵז, הוּא חוֹשֵׁשׁ.
אַבָּא, אוֹמֵר הוּא, אַבָּא הוּא גְּדִי,
וּגְדִי הוּא זוּזֵי וְזוּזֵי בִּכְדִי.
לְמַקֵּל הוּא קוֹרֵא: כֶּלֶב. כֶּלֶב יִרְדֹּף.
וְשׁוּנְרָא חָתוּל אוֹ נָמֵר אוֹ קוֹף.
מַלְאַךְ הַמָּוֶת שָׁחוֹט שָׁחוּט?
מִי הַשּׁוֹחֵט? הוּא שׁוֹאֵל, אֵיךְ נִחְיֶה
אִם אִישׁ לֹא יָמוּת?
הַאִם לֹא שָׂבַע? הַעוֹדוֹ רָעֵב?
הַזָּקֵן אוֹהֵב! אוֹהֵב! אוֹהֵב!

# BOOKS BY TUVIA RUEBNER

POETRY

*The Fire in the Stone* [האש באבן]   1957

*Poems Seeking Time* [שירים למצוא עת]   1961

*As Long As* [כל עוד]   1967

*Poems by Tuvia Ruebner* [שירים]   1970

*Unreturnable* [אין להשיב]   1970

*Midnight Sun* [שמש חצות]   1977

*A Graven and A Molten Image* [פסל ומסכה]   1982

*And Hasteneth to His Place* [ואל מקומו שואף]   1990

*Latter Day Poems* [שירים מאוחרים]   1999

*Almost a Conversation* [כמעט שיחה]   2002

*Nasty Children's Rhymes and More* [חרוזי ילדים קלוקלים ואחרים]   2004

*Traces of Days: New & Selected Poems 1957–2005*
[עקבות ימים: מבחר שירים]   2005

*Belated Beauty* [יופי מאוחר]   2009

*Contradictory Poems* [שירים סותרים]   2011

*Last Ones* [אחרונים]   2013

*The Crossroads* [פרשת הדרכים]   2015

*Still Before* [עוד לפני]   2017

*Seventeen* [שבע-עשרה]   2018

*From Here To: Selected Poems* [מכאן עד]   2018

*More No More* [עוד לא עוד]   2019

AUTOBIOGRAPHY

*A Short Long Life* [חיים ארוכים קצרים]   2006
   Published first in German (titled *Ein langes kurzes Leben*), and then in Hebrew.

PHOTOGRAPHY

*Everything that Came After* [כל מה שאחר כך]   2007

*This Too My Eyes Have Seen* [גם זו ראו עיני] – with poems   2008

CRITICAL MONOGRAPH

*Lea Goldberg*   1980

## POETRY COLLECTIONS IN GERMAN

*Wüstenginster,* translated by Efrat Gal-Ed and Christoph Meckel   1990

*Granatapfel*   1995

*Rauchvögel 1957–1997,* vol. 1   1998

*Stein will Fliessen*   1999

*Zypressenlicht 1957–1999,* vol. 2   2000

*Wer hält diese Eile aus*   2007

*Spätes Lob der Schönheit*   2010

*Lichtschatten*   2011

*In Vorbereitung: Wunderbarer Wahn*   2013

*Im halben Lich*   2016

## SELECTED TRANSLATIONS

### FROM HEBREW INTO GERMAN

*Im Wald und in der Stadt* [ביער ובעיר] by S.J. Agnon (in *Schalom: Erzählungen aus Israel*)   1964

*Der Treueschwur: Erzählung* [שבועת אמונים] by S.J. Agnon   1965

*Schira: Roman* [שירה] by S.J. Agnon   1998

*Der Vorabend: Erzählung* [עם כניסת היום] by S.J. Agnon   2004

*Erdichteter Mensch: Gedichte Hebräisch/Deutsch* [איש בדוי] by Dan Pagis   1993

### FROM GERMAN INTO HEBREW

*Fragments* by Friedrich Schlegel   1982

*Chapters* by Goethe   1984

*Essays* by Aryeh Ludwig Strauss   1984

*Man and Poetry* by Aryeh Ludwig Strauss (with Yedidya Peles)   1985

*An Introduction to Aesthetics* by Jean Paul   1985

*Poems* by Christoph Meckel (with Asher Reich)   2002

*Black-winged Angel* by Milan Richter   2005

## SELECTED EDITED COLLECTIONS

### IN HEBREW

*Hebrew Studies in Literature* by Aryeh Ludwig Strauss   1959

*Poems* by Lea Goldberg   1970

*Remains of Life* by Lea Goldberg (a posthumous collection)   1971

*The Collected Poems of Lea Goldberg* (Three volumes)   1973

*The Writings of Lea Goldberg* (Five volumes)    1972–79

*Plays* by Lea Goldberg    1979

*On the Aesthetic Education of Man in a Series of Letters* by Friedrich Schiller. Translated from German by Shimshon Eilat    1986

*The Surrealist Manifesto* by André Breton    1986

*On Modern Art* by Paul Klee. Translated from German by Shlomo Tanay    1987

*Something Will Be: Selected Poems of Paul Celan.* Translated by Ben-Zion Orgad    1987

*Plotinus's Aesthetics.* Translated from Greek, introduced and annotated by Natan Shpigel    1987

*Conversations with Kafka* by Gustav Janouch    1988

*From Lessing to Kafka* by Werner Kraft    1988

*On Dramatic Poetry* by John Dryden. Translated from English by David Eren    1988

*Baudelaire* by Walter Benjamin. Translated from German by David Eren    1989

*The Duende Game and Its Principles* by Frederico García Lorca. Translated from Spanish, annotated and introduced by Renee Litvin    1989

*The Devil in the Artists' Quarter* by Eliezer Steinman 1992

IN GERMAN

*Briefwechsel Martin Buber-Ludwig Strauss,* 1913–1953; edited by Tuvia Ruebner and Dafna Mach    1990

*Gesammelte Werke in vier Bänden / Ludwig Strauss;* edited by Tuvia Ruebner and Hans Otto Horch    1998–2001

# BOOKS BY RACHEL TZVIA BACK

POETRY

*Litany*   1995

*Azimuth*   2001

*The Buffalo Poems*   2003

*On Ruins & Return: Poems 1999–2005*   2007

*A Messenger Comes (Elegies)*   2012

*What Use is Poetry, the Poet is Asking*   2019

TRANSLATIONS

*Lea Goldberg: Selected Poetry & Drama* (play translation by T. Carmi)   2005

*Night, Morning: Selected Poems of Hamutal Bar-Yosef*   2008

*With an Iron Pen: Twenty Years of Hebrew Protest Poetry*   2009

*In the Illuminated Dark: Selected Poems of Tuvia Ruebner*   2015

*On the Surface of Silence: The Last Poems of Lea Goldberg*   2018

CRITICAL WORK

*Led by Language: The Poetry & Poetics of Susan Howe*   2001

# ACKNOWLEDGMENTS

I write these acknowledgments sitting in the spacious, sun-lit common room of Translation House Looren, overlooking Zurich Lake and the verdant hills and valleys all around. Happily, I begin my thank-yous here. I am deeply grateful to the team at Looren for the work-haven they sustain and nurture, and for their gracious help and kindness to me in all matters. I am grateful also to the team at Europäische Übersetzer-Kollegium in Straelen, Germany, where I completed a significant amount of the early work on this collection during a three-week winter residency. I am moved by the fashion in which both these institutions welcome translators from around the world to work in quiet and deep focus, and the fluid cross-linguistic, cross-border communities they make possible. These institutions are a model of important transnational cultural work that has the potential to make a difference in our divided world.

A great joy of completing this manuscript and having it accepted for publication by Hebrew Union College Press was knowing I would have the pleasure of working again with Sonja Rethy, managing editor of the press. I am profoundly grateful to Sonja for transforming the exacting work of manuscript-preparation into a pleasurable process. Sonja's patience, professionalism, keen ear, fierce intelligence and generosity of spirit quietly and certainly left their mark everywhere in this book.

Deep gratitude to David H. Aaron, co-director of HUC Press, for the invaluable notes on my translations that he offered, together with an anonymous second reader. This scholarly input not only made my renderings much better than they would have been otherwise, but also provided me with different perspectives on the poems, on their referenced sources, and on the Hebrew language all. I find myself always learning from David, as one does from true scholars; for the unmitigated pleasure of that learning, I am grateful.

I am wholly beholden to Tuvia Ruebner's Israeli editors, the poets Rafi Weichert and Liat Kaplan. Rafi Weichert edited *The Crossroads* (*Parashat Derachim*, published by Keshev Press) and was singularly instrumental in establishing for Ruebner a place in the canon of modern Hebrew poetry. Liat Kaplan edited *Still Before* (*Od Lifnei*) and *More No More* (*Od Lo Od*: both collections were published by Bialik Institute) and has been a vigorous champion of Ruebner's poetry for years. Both editors also immediately shared the digital Hebrew manuscripts of the collections included in this book, allowing this bilingual edition to move more quickly and easily into the world. I do not take that collegial consideration for granted and am very grateful.

I extend deep gratitude to Giddon Ticotsky for his gracious help at numerous junctures and for his great kindness in all matters. Thanks also to Raphaël Freeman for his elegant typesetting, and to Elena Barschazki for her cover design. Thanks as well to Mel Freilich for his gracious permission to use his photo of Ruebner, and to the editors of the following journals where some of these translations first appeared: *The Cincinnati Review, World Literature Today, Tablet* and *Forward*.

My penultimate thanks are for Galila Ruebner, pianist, and wife to Tuvia for 66 years. From the first time I visited the Ruebners in Kibbutz Merchavia, Galila welcomed me into their home; I am grateful to Galila for that immediate warmth and ensuing support. But beyond the personal, I am cognizant of the great debt all who love Ruebner's Hebrew poems owe Galila Ruebner. In the beginning of his Hebrew poetic career, it was Galila who put diacritics on and proofread all her husband's poems; as Hebrew is her native tongue and was not his, one cannot over-estimate the importance of that early input. Through the years, she was his most faithful reader and critic, offering unfailing support, and putting his artistic career above her own. To Galila, for making Ruebner's poems possible, gratitude is a small, but necessary, word.

I complete my work on this book a few months after Tuvia Ruebner's passing. I know the gift I was given in knowing him, in being embraced by him as his English language translator and also, eventually, as a friend. The visits to Merhavia with the old poet reciting his new poems and telling his stories were charmed hours, every one of them. I extend my gratitude into the world for this great gift. And now, with deep love intertwined with sorrow, from across the threshold, I thank Tuvia too.

*Rachel Tzvia Back*
*November 2019*